VICTIMOLOGY AND CRIMINAL LAW

Crime Precipitated or Programmed by the Victim

Edmundo Oliveira

University Press of America,® Inc.
Lanham · Boulder · New York · Toronto · Plymouth, UK

Copyright © 2008 by
University Press of America®, Inc.
4501 Forbes Boulevard
Suite 200
Lanham, Maryland 20706
UPA Acquisitions Department (301) 459-3366

Estover Road
Plymouth PL6 7PY
United Kingdom

Library of Congress Control Number: 2007938469
ISBN-13: 978-0-7618-3948-4 (paperback : alk. paper)
ISBN-10: 0-7618-3948-8 (paperback : alk. paper)

⊖™ The paper used in this publication meets the minimum
requirements of American National Standard for Information
Sciences—Permanence of Paper for Printed Library Materials,
ANSI Z39.48—1984

Contents

Topical Index

Preface

Victimology, as a field of scientific endeavor, has grown considerably during the last forty years. It has had considerable influence on the perception and appreciation of the experience the victim undergoes during and after the commission of the crime; on the recognition of the victim as worthy of services, assistance, compensation and restitution; on the need for reform of the penal law especially to correct the clear injustices of a system interested more in protecting the rights of the accused and of the convict than in allowing the victim a clear role and an active participation in the criminal justice process; on the academic and professional recognition of the victim as a major subject for research, theory development, and therapeutic interventions; and finally on the general awareness, appreciation and understanding of the victim by the media and the public in general.

This development and evolution of victimology has not been easy since it touches upon the complex web of values, beliefs, customs, mores, laws and behaviors that at times exist since time immemorial. Giving the victim his or her rightful recognition within the dynamics of a criminal event challenges and questions many of the perceptions, attitudes, values and systemic reactions of a vast number of people, officials, judges, police, prosecutors, lawyers, medical personnel, social workers, psychologists; a large number of institutions, from the criminal justice system in its various branches to social work, mental health, insurance, legislatures, the government, emergency services and crisis intervention; and the community at large.

Most of all, victimology forces us to re-examine our definitions of criminal and victim; our concepts and values about criminal responsibility, innocence and guilt, contributory behaviors or at least negligence, power and control, undue influence and duress. Victimology challenges key concepts that are at the core of our criminal law and of our understanding of vulnerability, responsibility, provocation, contribution, and shared culpability. It also forces us to re-examine our understanding and conception of roles, human relations, stereotypes and assumptions, the position of men and women relative to power and control over their lives, bodies, and behaviors. There is no question that the discussion of victim provocation versus vulnerability is one of the most delicate, controversial and politically charged ones, especially when it is related to men and women encounters and relations in an intimate or sexual context. The whole concept and laws related to sexual assault, rape, rape in marriage and domestic violence have been intensely questioned by the victimology movement, often challenging behavioral assumptions that placed the onus and responsibility for violent or forced sexual encounters onto the woman and her supposed seductive behavior, absolving men from any responsibility for their own violent, forceful or exploitative behavior. To blame a child victim of sexual attack or age-inappropriate sexual activities by describing the behavior of the men, often older, as responding to the female's seductive or "experienced" behavior was and still is often the norm, especially in some parts of the world. Even if it were true that a minor is maybe unwittingly seductive, it is still the responsibility of the older male to "know better" and to refrain from age-inappropriate or forced sexual activity.

Victimology has expanded considerably during the last 40 years and now encompasses rape and sexual assault, rape in marriage, domestic violence, date rape, child abuse and neglect, child sexual assault and incest, victimization of the elderly, compensation, restitution, victim-offender mediation and reconciliation, victim assistance services including assisting and orienting the victim through the criminal justice system, witness protection services, and more.

In this volume Professor Edmundo Oliveira first offers a clear, exhaustive and comprehensive overview of the historical, conceptual, legal and practice-oriented aspects of victimology. Then he especially focuses on psychology and penal law as they relate to the survivor of crime, highlighting themes of personal responsibility, provocation, precipitation, participation, and diminished responsibility. In chapter VII, the path to victimization, defined as "the trajectory followed by the author in the dynamics of developing a misdeed," is analyzed in detail. The various combinations of offender and victim interactions are illustrated with helpful and clear graphics. Repeat victimization is examined in depth in chapter VIII; victim precipitating or programming the crime in chapter

IX, and types of victims in chapter X. These themes—victim precipitation, provocation, vulnerability, shared responsibility, repeat victimization, victim typology—are controversial, delicate, difficult and even explosive. The women's movement especially has reacted negatively to any statement or analysis that reflects a stereotypical view of women as responsible for their sexual assault or for men-perpetrated violence in the family.

Too often, male values and perspectives have been translated into laws, both statutes and common law, that blame women, at times still children, for their victimization by men. Victimology has helped recognize this bias and correct it, placing the blame where it belongs with rare exceptions: on the male attacker.

Not everyone will agree with Prof. Oliveira's analysis, terminology and position on these issues but he must be recognized and given credit for addressing these difficult points, presenting his reasoned and considered opinion, and starting a dialogue, a discussion that may help clarify these challenging issues. They are still vexing and at times even a matter of life or death in some parts of the world.

Finally, Professor Oliveira addresses the victim specifically in Brazilian criminal law, a major contribution to the development and the influence of victimology in South America.

This book will no doubt greatly contribute to the growing body of scholarly literature on victimology particularly related to Latin American legal concepts and traditions. It fills a vacuum widely felt and advances the development of the field in Brazil and elsewhere. It is a remarkable work that represents the culmination of years of study, reflection, dialogue and will spur debate, discussion, and research on the basic concepts and elements of the victimological discourse and approach.

That Professor Oliveira has undertaken this difficult and challenging task is a testimony to his commitment to contribute to the scholarly and reasoned debate in the field, advance it to its ultimate frontier, and ensure that it is recognized as an important new area of study with important policy and legal implications.

Academics, practitioners, professionals, law enforcement, criminal justice, victim assistance personnel, criminal justice and law students will find this book quite useful as a springboard for enlightening and spirited debates and conversations that hopefully will also lead into action and intervention on behalf of the survivors of crime and for a clear and concise statement of various positions worldwide on victimology.

As the author himself says, "this book will yield good fruits . . . for the efficient application of criminal law in Brazil and . . . in the English-speaking countries." This is an ambitious agenda but doable, especially with the added focus on victimological themes spurred by the publication of this book. Survivors certainly deserve it!

Emilio C. Viano
Professor
American University
Washington DC

Introduction

This book was not produced in a flash. It was written, polished, organized and reorganized as I advanced in my studies and research over the years. 11 years were needed to complete the broadening of the victimological perspective that makes up the dynamic field of the conceptual approach related to the theory of crime precipitated or programmed by the victim, in terms of juridical-penal dogmatics and criminal phenomenology.

I initially focused on this theme as a small monograph presented at the VI International Symposium of Victimology, held at the University of Jerusalem, in Israel, in 1988. It was there that I personally met the American Marvin Wolfgang, then professor at the University of Philadelphia, who in 1956, coined, for the first time in the history of victimology, the expression "victim-precipitated crime," to refer to the deviance that expresses a direct relation between the victim and the delinquent.

The topic is one that genuinely brings together theoretical elevation and a significant degree of practical importance. A serious study of the victim, under the anthropological, psychic and social aspects is one of the great challenges that the third millennium poses for specialists in Criminal Sciences. Classifications of victims, based on observation and experience, have been replacing primitive classifications made with aprioristic and fanciful criteria, which are not confirmed by reality. Diagnosis and therapeutics are now being founded on evidence, finally brought together in the complex and modern Victimological Exam.

For the moment, the bibliography on the subject is scanty. Monographs on precipitation by the victim, both in Brazil and overseas, are mere essays, which, focus, furthermore, on only a few facets of this polyhedron which is the human being identified as a victim under Criminal Law.

Precisely with regard to the probable identity of some type of victim affected by a personality disorder, I sought a holistic view of the theme, both in its breadth and its scientific depth. Countless times it was necessary to return to the starting point, or at least to earlier positions, reexamine the material collected, decant and filter it, establish a confrontation between partial conclusions, correct and redo.

Criminal Law and Victimology were, for a long time, entirely separated compartments.

Currently, thanks to the studies of Augusto Balloni, Binyamin Mendelsohn, Denis Szabo, Elias Carranza, Elias Neuman, Emilio C. Viano, Georges Kellens, Hans Jescheck, Hans Schneider, Hans von Henting, Heber Soares Vargas, Jacques Farsedakis, José Luis de la Cuesta, Lola Aniyar de Castro, Luíz Rodriguez Manzanera, Marvin Wolfgang, Michael Hindelang, Mireille Delmas-Marty, Phillip Rapoza, Pierre-Henri Bolle, Reinhart Maurach, Vasile Stanciu, Severin Versele, Stéphan Parmentier and very many others, the two branches—Victimology and Criminal Law—are connected to the same trunk, which is that of crime, and defined by criminal law.

Victimologists and criminologists dedicate themselves to studying the polemical and intense issues raised by delinquency and the manner of looking at the delinquent in the context of humanity as a whole. This happens exactly because neither Victimology nor Criminal Law arises from *a priori* concepts. Instead, they are the products of refined observation and careful experience. They are informed by the conclusions of various sciences that study crime as a phenomenon, occurrence or fact, not as an abstraction, because it is something concrete, existential and historic.

This book, like any serious didactical work, is perfectible, and for this reason is the starting point for further and more in-depth work, especially if we consider that in certain concrete situations, one must consider not only the author of the crime, but the fact that the victim, even when innocent, may have the sensation of being an intruder. However, in many criminal cases in the forensic area he or she is seen as a stranger by the police and dealt with rudely, and viewed with indifference by the Courts, where a not uncommon tactic of the defendant's layer is to try to drag the victim into the mud or into a labyrinth of difficulties.

On the other hand, in the fields of relativity of guilt and interpersonal dialectics, the roles may be inverted, considering that it is possible to determine the impact produced by the victim, at the moment when he or she goes beyond the limits and becomes the dominant agent of the crime, when, under any pretext, she or he provides the means of intervention or participation, in the sense of precipitating or programming, with her or his own style, the coordinates of his victimization, becoming the bait of an attempt, or serving as ammunition to attract even the aggressor's imaginary plexus, just as sheep attract wolves in the field. Thus, we may say that, in the same measure that the criminal patiently models his or her victim, the victim may also model the criminal, mainly when, consistently with this performance, she or he bursts forth prepared to commit any sort of crime.

I trust that this book will yield good fruits for the pragmatic prestige and the efficient application of Criminal Law in Brazil and now in the English-speaking countries.

Edmundo Oliveira

Chapter 1

Historical Foundations

Theoretical Presuppositions in Victimology

The optimism brought into the world by the Illuminists, who supposed that they could achieve domination of the universe through Science, disappeared from the moment that people perceived that in order to fulfill themselves and be happy, they would have to focus more on themselves than on the external environment. Romanticism clearly depicted the tedium that had taken hold of everyone at the end of the XVII century and the first half of the XIX century. This was the "*mal de siècle*," so well depicted by Henri Stendahl in *The Black and the Red*; it was the "pain of the world," which had Johan Goethe and Friedrich Schiller as its prophets and Lord Byron as its greatest interpreter. It was perceived that the conquest of the physical world means nothing when human beings do not take care of their own selves, of their personalities, and not aspire to fulfill themselves entirely, body and soul, to discover and follow the best sense of life.

Another frequent observation is that of the variety of reactions of those who live in the same environment and are struck by the same disasters and misfortunes. At the moment when these lines are being written, the world is undergoing a terrible economic crisis. Thousands of people lose their jobs every day. And each person reacts differently than the others. While some face the difficulties and bear the disaster or misfortune heroically, others, at the first crisis, head towards crime as the means for providing their subsistence. How complex is the human soul! What Shakespeare is capable of fully understanding it?

It is possible to conclude, then, that aggressiveness, while as necessary as sex is for reproduction, is not compulsively destructive. Unless a biological revolution occurs to change human personality as a species, it is utopian to hope that someday there will be a society without struggle and without competition. In the same way that a child needs to be aggressive to become an independent adult, adults need to free part of their aggressive potential to maintain their own singularity and autonomy.

No one expects that education and cultural progress will be able to abolish or even to substantially soften the human tendency towards competitive struggle, since the aggressive impulse that leads to war and destruction equally underlies the impulse toward independence and personal fulfillment. The desired balance will be achieved when we discover ways by which humans can compete and struggle, without exterminating themselves or their fellows.

Humans have again occupied the center of scientific concerns, and in light of this, students of Victimology are increasingly directing their efforts towards personality data revealed from the repercussions of genetic makeup, temperament disposition, character formation, environmental adaptation, reactions derived from the influence of physical factors on psychic factors and vice-versa. Herein lies the great merit of victimological studies and research: to enable a systematic and coherent reflection on the human individual who is capable of heroic sublimation or criminal degradation with poisonous fruits.

From the historical point of view, among primitive peoples, the victim was the animal destined to be sacrificed to appease divine wrath or offered in thanksgiving for benefits received. The Latin language employed, in the first case, the word *hostia,* and in the second, *victima* (Mason, 1962, p.1).

Criminal Law is greatly interested in Victimology, exactly because it deals with every characteristic of the victim. Often, in order to understand the psychology referring to the author as protagonist of the crime, it is essential to understand the sociology inherent to the victim's personality.

Seeking to broadly study questions related to the victim, Victimology appeared shortly after World War II, not only to take care of victims of crimes, but also to deal with their relationship with the delinquent, that is, the aggressor,[1] in the complexity of the criminal phenomenon that involves interpersonal dialectic.

It is still somewhat early to issue a definitive concept for Victimology and to draw out its boundaries and contours. In fact, there is controversy as to whether it should be considered a section of empirical Criminology or a Science in its own right, which who encompass medical, biological, psychological and sociological issues.

In our understanding it is difficult to fit all of the victimological themes within Criminology, and for this reason we side with the philosophical segment that considers Victimology as a Science, which, like all others in their inaugural phase, stumbles somewhat as it gathers its instruments and begins to affirm itself. Mathematics began in the most empirical manner possible, with people using their fingers to count. From that point, many centuries were to pass before the Sumerians invented the counting tables. Chemistry began as Alchemy, which, mixed with superstition, sought to discover the elixir for long life. Physics took its first steps with the basic elements of mechanics. Agronomy started off in very rudimentary fashion and grew to include draining of swamps and irrigation of deserts. Astronomy was Astrology to begin with, cultivated with a view to predicting the future. Egyptian medicine saw disease as the work of the Devil (Dampier, 1957, pp. 1-4).

The Victim and the Criminal Phenomenon

Victimology arose exactly out of the martyrdom suffered by the Jews in the concentration camps commanded by Adolf Hitler, with the notable Israeli lawyer, Binyamim Mendelsohn, Emeritus Professor of the Hebrew University of Jerusalem being recognized as the founder of Victimological doctrine. Its first historical landmark was a presentation given by Mendelsohn at the University of Bucharest in 1947, his famous Conference of *A New Horizon in Biopsyhcosocial Science: Victimology* (Lopez-Rey, 1978, pp. 145-149).

The essential peculiarity in Victimology resides in demolishing the apparent simplicity regarding victim and showing, instead, that study of the victim is a labyrinthine task that expresses considerable complexity, both at the individual level and in the meanderings of life shared for the common welfare in the social environment.

Although Mendelsohn is honored by most specialists as the founder of systematized Victimological doctrine, one may not ignore the existence of various previously disseminated studies with significant contents.

There is, for example, the record of Professor Marvin Wofgang, in a work particularly directed towards *victim-precipitated homicide*, in which the notes that Gabriel Tarde, in his work *Penal Philosophy*, whose first edition was published in Paris in 1890, criticized the fact that legislation was excessively directed towards premeditation of the crime by the delinquent, and gave little attention to motives indicating a significant interrelation between victim and offender (Tarde, 1890, *apud* Wolfgang, 1957, p.2).

Wolfgant noted also the brilliant satirical essay of the writer Thomas Dequincey, who much earlier had published in London in 1827, *On Murder as One of the Fine Arts*, describing the actions of certain persons who, being wealthy and having amassed countless material goods, cared little about the moral concerns that people should have on the personal and moral level. Consequently, given their lack of care in protecting their goods and themselves, these persons would become the artifices of their own extermination, with exposure to high risks, given their characteristic way of living and acting. Dequincey was anticipating the modern definition, which highlights behavioral duality as one of the most significant and confluent particularities in the attitudes of many victims (Dequincy, 1827, *apud* Wolfgang, 1957, pp. 9-11).

The collection of works related to the literature on victims is immense and citations of cases and research involving the theme have often illustrated books on Criminal Law and Criminology since the beginning of the XX century.

It is worth remembering, that Hans Gross, in 1901, in Germany, wrote about the credulity of fraud victims, a concern echoed by Edwin Sutherland, who, in 1920 in the United States, wrote an interesting opuscule about the victim who can contribute with his own bad faith to the fraud of swindling, which led Willy Callewaert in France to propose a thesis on the "victim of his own dishonesty" (Callewaert, 1959, pp. 613-614). In Germany, Ernest Roesner, in 1936 and 1938, published two studies on homicides related to their victims, based on statistics of condemned criminals serving prison sentences (Wolfgang, 1957, 99. 9-11). In 1941 it was the Italian Georges Romanos who released a commentary on victims of indecent assault, very well remembered by Eduardo Mayr in *Atualidade Vitimológica* (Mayr, 1990, p. 12).

Luigi Pirandello was one of the great Italian dramatists who knew how to develop in the theater the complexities of individual motivations and the personality disassociation caused by ideas and beliefs that alienated behavior in the social life. In his masterpiece *Henry IV,* premiering in Paris in 1923, Pirandello analyzes the question of a man who consciously chose insanity as the solution to his problems. The main character goes mad and begins to believe he is Henry IV, and his family, to comfort him, begins to treat him as if he really were the King, giving him a castle, honors and all of the attention due to a Monarch, so that he will not bother anyone. The character one day finds himself cured of his madness, but the life he has been living is agreeable, that he decides to say nothing to his family; he begins to feign insanity and continues as "King Henry IV." This approach has received considerable attention due to real-life facts, in which criminal dynamics lead to a characterological study of victimal perigosity (Delgado, 1966, pp. 131-132).

As a result of the milestone that the Binyamin Mendelsohn Conference of 1947 has presented for new technical knowledge about the victim as a person, important contributions have since appeared elucidating details, which, in some form, indicate a link with topics in Victimology with the scientific environment.

By the way, Emilio C. Viano, Professor at American University, in the United States, founded the first International Journal of Victimology, published the first series of Volumes on Victimology, and organized a series of international meetings, conferences and workshops that greatly contributed to the development and growth of the field.

Selective Nature of Sentiment in Victimology

Karl Menninger, one of the most talented researchers into delinquent personality in the field of psychoanalysis, writing in Germany in 1947 in *On Man against Himself,* presented exams done on persons who had attempted suicide, acting to seek and create opportunities for their own deaths, stimulated by the unconscious dynamization of absolutely intolerable conflicts. Menninger also dealt with cases of self-blaming victims, and self-punitive conduct, episodes that lead to the danger of *lost identity phenomenon*[2], which leads the victim to operate a *projective identity*, i.e., to project onto another his or her own reality. This would be the case of a person who, unconsciously or with a certain degree of consciousness, sees in the thief her or his own intimate affective need for owning something similar, and thus allows him or herself to be robbed. In another possibility, there is the example of a person who is aggressive against his or her own self or who attacks someone who causes her or him to have destructive or repulsive sentiments (Seeling, 1956, pp. 92-93).

Regarding sensations produced by conduct leading to responses driven by repulsive sentiments, Professor Godofredo Telles Júnior offers an excellent explanation:

"Sentiment is the psychic disposition, the state of the soul in which we place ourselves, in relation to a given object, after we have judged it."

We judge an object. We note that if serves, does not serve or hinders our mental disposition, related to that object, after that verification.

Every sentiment, as with every feeling of pleasure, pain or disdain, is an effective phenomenon, but the sentiment, unlike what occurs with sensations, is always an affective expression of one or several judgments.

There is a clear difference between the affective sensation and the sentiment.

The affective sensation is directly tied to the sensorial impression, without interference from any thought. Pleasure and pain are pleasure and pain, regardless of the opinion of the person experiencing them. One who is burned has the painful feeling of the burn, regardless of any meditations upon the fact.

Sentiment, however, is not a sensation in the body. It is really a state of spirit, resulting from a judgment regarding a fact or a thing.

The facts or things that are objects of our judgments may be convenient or inconvenient, useful or harmful; it matters little. What is certain is that related to a given object, we will have a given feeling, according to how we judge that the object will serve, not serve or hinder our purposes, whatever they may be, be they legitimate or not.

A student will have a sentiment of sadness when thinking about a failing grade on a test. An artist will have a sentiment of wonder when faced with a landscape that is the stuff of dreams. A thief will have a sentiment of joy upon discovering, under the doormat, the key to the door he or she was planning to break in through. In these three examples, as with all cases, sentiment is the result of judgment.

One might object that certain sentiments contradict reason and are thus not the product of any judgment. It has been said many times that "the heart has reasons that reason does not know." Such an argument would be impeccable, if the judgment to which we are referring were always made in relation to assets with absolute and invariable values. It so happens, however, that such a judgment is relative, it is contingent, it is personal, because it is made only related to ends effectively and actively sought by the one formulating it, without consideration for the real value of these same ends. It is a judgment made exclusively through *reference systems* accepted by the person doing the judging.

If an object is judged convenient and adequate to the ends sought by the judger, whatever they may be, the sentiment resulting from such a judgment will be a *sentiment of attraction* for said object. Otherwise, the sentiment will be a *sentiment of repulsion*.

As a consequence of the relativity of those judgments, a person who adopts different systems of reference can make more than one judgment regarding the same object. Evidently, an object may be judged an appropriate means for achieving a given end, and, at the same time, be considered an obstacle to achieving another end.

From these disparate judgements, different sentiments will inevitably be aroused: the first a *sentiment of attraction* and the second a *sentiment of repulsion*. Besides, who does not know, from personal experience, the clash of sentiments? We simultaneously desire and repudiate the same thing; we desire it for one reason and repudiate it for another.

As a flagrant example of this clash of sentiments, we may sight the frequent cases of alcoholics who hate the drink that they love. Psychiatrists and criminologists know that there are not infrequent cases of women madly in love with the men they most detest. It is not rare, in fact, to have the most ardent love coexisting in the same heart with the most intense hatred.

There are two types of sentiment, according to the sense of the judgment preceding them. As we have just seen, the sentiments may be *attractive* or *repulsive*.

Attractive sentiments include happiness, desire, love, friendship, empathy, admiration and enthusiasm. *Repulsive sentiments* include sadness, antipathy, enmity, hatred, disdain, despeito, disgust, fear, shame.

Therefore, attractive and repulsive, *the sentiments lead people to action. Human beings act according to their sentiments.* " (Telles Júnior, 1974, 99. 188-190).

The *Stockholm Syndrome*

To demonstrate the extent to which human beings habitually act according to their sentiments, be they attractive or repulsive, one may point out the example of behavioral variation that has been termed the *Stockholm*

Syndrome, which manifests itself by means of two types of symptoms (Lopez, 1977, p. 66):

   a. feeling of empathy, on the part of the victim, towards the aggressor;
   b. feeling of empathy the aggressor has toward the victim.

The *Stockholm Syndrome* may accompany incidents of sexual crime, armed robbery, kidnap, swindling, blackmail and domestic violence.

Particularly with regard to domestic violence of the husband against the wife, there are cases in which she, even though repressed, subjugated and mistreated, nourishes a paradoxical affective relationship with her companion, choosing to accommodate herself to silence and not denounce the aggressor, with whom she continues to live. Thus, the woman enters a state of defense with passive resistance, trying to guide the situation without losing identification with the loved one, many times even blaming the society in which she lives for the torments suffered.

A notorious crime scene from the City of São Paulo illustrates the *Stockholm Syndrome* formula.

Patrícia Abravanel, daughter of the well-know television magnate Sílvio Santos, was kidnapped on August 21, 2001. After seven days in captivity, those responsible for the abduction negotiated the ransom, received five hundred thousand reals and released the victim. A few hours after being released, "a smiling Patrícia talked to the press, said she had been treated very well in captivity, forgave the kidnappers, preached social justice, income distribution and condemned corruption in the Country." (*Isto É* magazine, issue 1666, 2001, pp. 26-27).

From whence does this phenomenon called the *Stockholm Syndrome* come, after all?

Andrés Montero, Spanish professor and psychologist, studied the outcome of events labeled with the title of *Stockholm Syndrome,* in the circumstances in which the person assumes a differentiated posture in the coordinates of his or her own victimization (Montero, 1999, pp. 4-5). The first event of this nature occurred in the City of Stockholm, Sweden, when six men invaded the Swedish Credit Bank to take money, and for several days kept as hostages the bank employees who had been working there.

After the robbery, the great surprise was the unanimous attitude of the hostages; they showed empathy towards the robbers and all testified in their favor in the courts. One newspaper even published a photograph showing, at the moment when they were being freed, a bank employee kissing one of the robbers.

Another case christened with the title of *Stockholm Syndrome*, with notable repercussions in Europe, was that of the attitude of a diplomat from the German Embassy, kidnapped in Stockholm in 1975. When returned, he declared his open empathy with the kidnappers, who belonged to the German *Baader-Meinhoff* terrorist movement.

In the international press, the events related to the kidnapping of Patricia Campbell Hearst, daughter of Randolph Hearst, one of the most eminent business leaders in the American media sector, received enormous attention.

Patricia, then 19 years old, was kidnapped on February 3, 1974, by the terrorist group *Symbionese Liberation Army*, which preached a social revolution in favor of needy people. The group decided it would only free Patricia after proof that her father Randolph Hearst was offering high quality food to all of the poor people in California. Randolph Hearst followed the order and actually spent around two million dollars in distributing food for several days, paying around seventy dollars to each person served.

As Patricia herself related in her autobiography, the psychic dynamics developed involving her growing admiration for the complacency of her torturers, who impressed her with their determined proposals for life and their conviction that they were doing right.

In two months of captivity, Patricia Hearst was transformed. She one day wrote a letter to her parents, saying that she had decided to stay with the kidnappers, and was thus renouncing her name and calling herself Tania, the pseudonym employed by Tamara Bunge, Che Guevara's companion.

On April 15, 1974, during a bank robbery, the cameras in the Hibernia Bank of San Francisco—a bank belonging to the parents of Patricia's best friend—captured images of the robbers. One of them was Patricia Hearst, carrying a machine gun.

She continued her involvement in the violent actions of the *Symbionese Liberation Army* until May of 1976, when she was finally arrested.

In her defense strategy, Patricia alleged that she had joined the group because she could no longer stand the pressure of remaining isolated in a room for several weeks, and of being a victim of sexual abuse. That was why she had the choice of joining the terror group or dying. Sentenced by the California Justice System to 10 years of imprisonment, Patricia Hearst served only 23 months of prison, thanks to a pardon granted by Jimmy Carter, President of the United States.

From the psychological point of view, the *Stockholm Syndrome* is considered one of the multiple emotional responses that may embed in the energy of a helpless or vulnerable person, who coexists or spends a certain amount of time with the aggressor. It is, however, an attitude that develops in a progressive manner, absorbed by the increase of a certain dosage of affective current, produced in an automatic manner and never forced.

Such a reaction is mainly explained by the prolonged contact between victim and aggressor. Martin Symonds calls this phase "frozen fright," as if the aggressor were to "put the victim into a freezer." The victim may initially feel intense fear, but knows how to hide it, stays calm, tries to cooperate with the captor and goes along obeying orders, gradually reducing the shock of the crime (Symonds, 1980, pp. 36-38).

Traumatic situations can lead the victim to develop defense mechanisms as a means of safeguarding personal integrity. Psychoanalysis explains this as a *reactive formation*, which consists of keeping the impulse that is undesired by the ego unconscious. The person begins to exhibit behavior that is diametrically opposed to the previously internalized social rules, when confronted by a psychological disturbance that involves violation of his or her personality. Thus, instead of a repulsive or hostile reaction, the victim paradoxically manifests cordial and affective behavior, going so far as to markedly express feelings of gratitude and submission. The *Stockholm Syndrome* can have a prolonged duration, depending on the recovery process that leads to an *ad integrum* return of the affected mental state (Dewald, 1973, p. 30).

There is no doubt that in many situations, such as the events following a kidnapping, the victim consciously tries to disguise or manipulate a certain control over the situation, not only to reduce the impacts of aggression and threat, but also to obtain some benefits: gestures of mercy and support that will guarantee her or his survival. This typical scenario of diverting attention should not be understood as being a case of *Stockholm Syndrome*.

To detect and diagnose the *Stockholm Syndrome,* it is thus essential that the following concurrent prerequisites be observed:

a. the victim progressively assumes a distinct identification of attraction, esteem, empathy, friendship and understanding with regard to the aggressor's attitudes, behavior, styles of thinking and acting;

b. initial expressions of gratitude, as a result of having escaped the crisis, are prolonged over time, so that the victim does not complain of any aggression, violence or mistreatment by the aggressor;

c. the victim, instead of attacking the aggressor, provides a degree of justification for certain forms of delinquent conduct, and instead, criticizes lack of action by government leaders, socioeconomic inequalities and injustices towards the less-favored.

Thus, it may be seen that in terms of Victimology, the *Stockholm Syndrome* represents a significant aspect of the dimensions that individualize the victim's personality, when faced with the complexities of the criminal phenomenon, exposing human sentiments in their most varied nuances.

The Special Case of a Kidnapping Victim with a Diagnosis of *Stockholm Syndrome*

Endogenous Effects

- The signs and symptoms of this syndrome that is motivated by kidnapping were diagnosed in 1973, by F. Ochberg, in Sweden, focusing on the famous robbery with hostage-taking at the Credit Bank in the City of Stockholm (Lopez and Bornstein, 1995, pp. 111-117).

- Post-Traumatic Stress Syndrome (PTS) was identified at that time as an endogenous complication frequently occurring in hostage situations.

- That syndrome manifests itself in paradoxical behavior that can perturb the lives of the hostages and their families, as *indirect victimization* or even *multiple victimization*.

- The frequency of the syndrome tends to diminish, after it is well known to the public in general and to the terrorists themselves, with medical prophylactic indications being important for this purpose.

Development of a Kidnapping/Hostage Taking Event

Whatever may be its typical configuration, as an event directed towards depriving a victim of liberty, a kidnapping develops in four phases summarized in the table below:

a. Moment of capture
    *   fear, confrontation with death;
    *   discouragement, anxiety, confusion, somatic distress.
b. Duration of the kidnapping
    *   dehumanization;
    *   doubting the captors' word;
    *   the kidnapping is a commercial value, varying according to development of negotiations;
    *   adaptation to the situation;
    *   specific personal mechanisms that induce paradoxical schemes between those involved in the kidnapping.
c. Being freed
    *   tension, danger, humiliation;
    *   recrudescence of anxiety (human shield);
    *   feeling of guilt, especially in a case where a single hostage has been released.
d. Exposure to after-effects
    *   post-traumatic stress (PTS);
    *   depression;
    *   *Stockholm Syndrome.*

Faces of the Pathology

The factors that induce Post-Traumatic Stress (PTS) are constantly present during the execution and consummation of a kidnapping.

Occurrence of the *Stockholm Syndrome* depends on defense mechanisms that emerge from the victim.

*   *Feeling of neediness in relation to society*. Neediness in relation to society (The providing State) updates the need for a real father. The apparently all-powerful kidnapper may substitute the image of the ideal father.
*   *Regressive phenomena*. These are the result of the victim's circumstance of total dependence (for food, for natural necessities, etc.) in relation to the kidnapper. This is a humili-

ating situation that reinforces the feeling of paternal power and the emergence of paradoxical defense mechanisms.

- *Process of identification with the aggressor.* Identification leads to introjection, leading the individual to assume some characteristic of the aggressor's personal nature.
- *Group feeling.* The kidnappers and their victims are placed in an exceptional situation, living together in extreme circumstances. The entire group feels menaced by a hostile environment. If positive contacts are established amongst themselves, a feeling of relief and cohesion makes an excellent defense matrix for all those involved. This is the experience that Psychology calls a *"feeling of collective illusion."* From then on, hostages and kidnappers have a common (ideal) objective: recovering their freedom.

Other peculiarities are pointed out:

a. the aggressors generally have a minimum of ideological certainty that justifies their conduct;
b. profound antagonism, such as racism or some other type of discrimination, does not become evident;
c. the victim who has undergone kidnapping always ignores the problems caused by the *Stockholm Syndrome* disruptions.

The Outcome, At the Critical Moment

The fragile stability organized by the individual or group defense, during the negotiation phase, especially if it is prolonged, is brutally tested when the final outcome is near, exacerbating the group's psychological tension (mortal risk). This explains certain paradoxical reactions the victims display towards their *liberators*. This is the key moment, when specific action by the victim may perform an essential preventive role.

Clinical Situation of the Stockholm Syndrome *During the Kidnapping*

Characterization of Three Orders of Symptoms

Strentz (1982, pp. 49-51) detailed three orders of symptoms, which, according to J. Bigot, are related to a scheme of *paradoxical behavior* by the victims and their kidnappers. The three orders of symptoms are:

a. feeling of empathy on the part of the hostages towards their captors;
b. negative feeling by the hostages in relation to authorities and the forces of order (Government, Police and Courts);
c. feeling of reciprocal empathy between hostages and kidnappers.

Paradoxical Behavior

Aspects of the specific hostage-kidnapper relationship:

a. lack on physical violence on the part of the kidnappers;
b. establishment of positive contact between the two parties.

The *Stockholm Syndrome* may only occur if there is establishment of interpersonal relations. In this regard, the duration of the kidnapping and its motives, clarified during the period of being together, are determining factors.

It is at this moment that remarkable group phenomena are established, according to reports on the attitudes of terrorists who isolate the hostages who are to be executed.

Evolution of Disturbance

The lives of the hostages may be left in complete disarray. They may begin to question all of the values that they had conceived of or believed in before the kidnapping, which may bring about serious consequences in their personal, family and social lives, with visible after-effects:

a. depression, which may be accompanied by feelings of guilt;
b. post-traumatic stress (PTS).

The Core of the Crisis in the Stockholm Syndrome

The Negotiation Exercise

The figure of the *technician-negotiator*, with knowledge of police techniques, is highly significant.

In the United States, the CIA and FBI are proposing specific training for their negotiator agents (Bargainer Police). The Neurolinguistic Program (NLP) is part of this proposal and is a technique for analyzing the ways in which a person communicates, enabling an understanding of that person's subjective experience. Analysis of behavioral modifications is essential (respiratory rhythm, muscular tension, intonation, etc.). The time factor works in favor of the negotiator, who can adapt scientifically to the aggressors mode of communication, thus increasing the changes of success with this strategy.

The purpose of the negotiation is to invert the relation of precarious force between the authorities and the delinquents. In this psychological clash, the negotiator seeks to move the adversary towards conciliation, or, better still, towards surrender. The goal, then, is not to kill the kidnapper but to avoid the death of the victim.

The Different Types of Negotiation

a. *Difficult negotiation*
When the kidnapper presents a serious mental disturbance, supporting his or her absolute conviction:

- with a psychotic disturbance;
- with a paranoid disturbance.

b. *Possible negotiation*
When the kidnapper has an interest in the success of the negotiations:

- the kidnapper is protecting her or his escape with a hostage;
- abduction in the midst of a mutiny or rebellion;
- kidnapper in a depressed state, seeking to attract attention to his or her case, exposing personal difficulties;
- kidnapper under effect of drugs;
- kidnapper defending an ideological cause, as happens with terrorist acts.

c. *Causal negotiation*
- conduct by a kidnapper with a psychopathic deviation;
- attempted suicide due to guilt feelings or to express a heroic attitude (the kidnapper wishes to die with a gun in her or his hand.

Stereotype of Delinquent/Victim Interaction

The weight of interaction or participation by the victim in producing the crime, which is capable of generating deviant behavior in the other person, converting the potential delinquent into a real delinquent, is a notably important criminological category in the juridical-criminal context of the forms of interaction between delinquent and victim.

In 1948 at Yale University in the United States, Hans von Henting published his work *The Criminal and His Victim*, where we find the first outline of a systematic study on the contribution of Psychology towards examining the "offender-victim" relation in producing the crime. Henting's teachings were extremely important in eliminating the thesis that reduces the victim's role to the condition of passive receiver of the wrongful action, when, in fact, he or she can represent a minimal, medium or notable function in generating the crime and even reveal, through her or his characteristic psychological type, a special inclination towards victimhood (Henting, 1948, pp. 408-413).

Adopting a distinct approach to this subject, the Belgian professor Severine Versele projected the conception of "native-born victim" in referring to types of persons who were constitutionally predestined to be victims and who can thus be identified, by any impulse, in unpredictable circumstances (Versele, 1962, p. 596).

As we have already indicated, Hans von Henting, advancing in his studies at Yale University, described the "victim by latency or tendency," one who has a special disposition or inclination to be converted into an object for all sorts of catastrophes or criminal actions, given a predisposition or vocation to those effects in his or her personality. This is a person who is not born a victim, but nonetheless suffers a reduction in her or his organic resistance due to a combination of forces of a biological disposition or mesological linkage, forces which can alter the rhythm of conduct and reduce critical powers and decisions when faced with facts and attitudes (Henting, 1962, 284-288).

The Venezuelan professor Lola Aniyar de Castro comments that "to speak, as was spoken of a natural-born criminal, and now of a natural-born victim expresses a concept that leads to the excesses of a witch hunt, in other words, of a doctrinal anachronism, given that even in relation to persons who are not normal, may we say that they were dragged along by irresistible forces to be converted into victims." Lola Aniyar de Castro adds that "perhaps the only natural-born victim we may conceive of would be Jesus Christ, who, as a Spiritual Messiah, came into the world to suffer resignedly until being murdered, giving his life to free and save humanity." (Castro, 1969, pp. 63-64).

We accept the typology of **victim by latency or tendency**, as well as the typology of **criminal by tendency**, but not the theory of **natural-**

born victim, nor the theory of **natural-born criminal**, since no one is born inexorably fated to be a victim or criminal. One may, in fact, be born with a predisposition, resulting from a certain biological or psychological weakness that gives a person a propensity both towards crime and towards becoming a victim of oneself or of others. Nonetheless, this does not mean predestination or congenital vocation.

The Italian doctor Cesare Lombroso recognized the existence of the natural-born criminal and described his morphological characteristics (Lombroso, 1876, pp. 21-92). However, later studies have disproved him. When he died, the Italian friar Agostino Gemelli dedicated a study to him: *I Funeralli di um Nomo i di una Dottrina* (Gemelli, 1948, pp. 74-85). Perhaps a better title would have been "The funerals of a genius and a mistake," since geniuses can also be negligent (*"Quandoque bonus Dormitat Homerus,"* says Quintus Horatius in *Poetic Art,* verse 359).

Regarding Cesare Lombroso, Professor Edmundo Mezger has written:

> Notwithstanding the fact that it cannot be demonstrated that the natural-born delinquent is a genuine human species, Lombroso's theory is also important in our days, since it was the first to, in a clear and determined fashion, promote and attempt to bring about a scientific-causal consideration of the transgression and a political-criminal treatment of the delinquent problem, supported by said theory. We cannot do without such a scientific-natural complement to the judicial side of this problem. Precisely if we highlight clearly and precisely the judicial-positive character of the concept of transgression and its historical-positive delimitation, and, finally, change because of circumstances of place and time, that which is considered delinquent, we shall have to demand, on the other hand, an exact scientific-experimental investigation of that phenomological sphere, which, as previously enunciated, was the object of a normative deliberation. For without a knowledge of the object on which the norm will need to act, it is not possible to generically have a normative function that will be appropriate to the inclination of the object and in harmony with its reality.[3]

Professor Geraldo Vasconcelos, in his book *Medicina Legal Criminológica,* expanded on recognition of the importance of Lombroso's work:

> Lombroso's merit was this: that of having led to a more modern and scientific conclusion of proceeding in accordance with the virtuous mean, abandoning petrified positions defended with antagonistic obsti-

nacy—always erroneous in its dogmatic rigidity—to move towards a position that is more realistic and amenable towards human truth, in which mean must be duly appreciated and, as a person, carefully examined as to the influences he may have suffered from his environment and from his own constitution.[4]

Due to his having evaluated criminals who carried bloodthirsty instincts, related to atavistic regression, Cesare Lombroso suffered criticism. But he never forgot to recognize the importance of sociological data in the notion of transgression, so much so that he attached great importance to crime prevention, noting, for this purpose, the need for education and instruction.

Professor Roberto Lyra, after noting that Gabriel Tarde asked Lobroso for his indulgence, expressed himself in this manner:

There is no need for tolerance for someone who, as Lombroso did, was self-critical before he was critical. Love for science—always austere, solid, fertile—inspired him towards probity in making retractions and towards an eagerness for overcoming errors. When he authorized the 5th edition of the *Experimental Treatise on the Delinquent Man,* Lombroso wrote: "The more I ascend along the path, as someone who, higher up, sees farther, I see ever more clearly the gaps." That is why he recognized that the first idea, as imperfect, as improvised as it is, is modified and transformed.[5]

To summarize: natural-born delinquent, no; delinquent due to tendency, yes. No person is born with a criminal inheritance, but only with the probability of practicing some anti-social act, as we will demonstrate in the chapter regarding the "tendency or inclination towards crime."

Victimodogmatics

Highlighting all the nuances of Criminal Law in which the victim's conduct has a specific significance, has opened up spaces for constructing modern *Victimodogmatics*. Establishing the greater or lesser contribution of the victim in the process of configuring the crime, with a emphasis on dogmatic valuing of the victim's behavior, is all placed within the context of *Victimodogmatics*. (Cancio Meliá, 1998, p. 23).

Victimodogmatics has drawn the attention of doctrine and jurisprudence towards a more in-depth examination related to the characteristics inherent to the reasons behind each criminal event. The effort becomes then, to attribute punishment to the author in the fairest way, without forgetting the possible identification of co-liability for the victim, or even her or his full self-liability, caught up in the web that brings about his or her own misfortune, a possibility that might lead to the exemption of culpability for the author, to the extent of his or her blame, as protagonist of the injury or exposure to danger of a determined judicial asset.

The finding of self-liability of the victim, in various events, is expanding the importance of the Principle of the *Subsidiary Nature of Criminal Law*, considering that the production of a fact, due to the risk of precipitation or programming of the crime by the victim, may bring about the non-recognition of culpability of the author (Wemmers, 2003, pp. 40-41), as occurs in countless crimes that are culpable or practiced with malice.

Notes

1. In Latin, the *victimarius*, the servant of the ancient Priests, who immolated or sacrificed victims among the pagans, at the end of the ancient Roman Empire. In the victimological sense, the aggressor is the one who produces the victim's damage or suffering. Other designations express the following qualities:

Victimology is the overall study of the victim.

Victimize is to convert or reduce someone to the condition of victim.

Victimizing is that which has the capacity to victimize.

Victimization is the effect of the act of victimizing.

Victimogenous is that which may produce victimization.

Victimizable is a person capable of being a victim.

Victimal is the circumstance that characterizes the state or situation of being a victim.

Victimological is everything related to understanding the typical or specific aspects inherent to Victimology.

Victimality represents the total of victimizations that arise in a specific conjuncture, put into effect in a given time and place. The term *victimality* is in counterpoint to the expression *criminality*, which is the set of antisocial conduct and actions that indicate the volume of crimes within a time and space limit;

Victimarius, in the original Latin sense was the servant of the ancient priests, whose duty it was to immolate, that is, to light the fire under the victim to sacrifice it until death. In the victimological sense, the *victimarius*, termed *aggressor* in this book, is one producing any time of damage, suffering or hardship for the victim.

2. With regard to this subject, the psychiatrist David Abrahamsen, responsible for examining Mark David Chapman, who ended John Lennon's life on December 8, 1980, reached the conclusion that the fact that Chapman signed the name of John Lennon, in the work log when he left his job as a security guard, is evidence that Chapman was losing what still remained of his fragile sense of personal identity. At the same time he maintained a superidentification with Lennon, he was openly competing with him. By killing Lennon, Chapman intended to find a substitute for his own suicide. He thus allowed himself to be dominated by an illusion and incorporated Lennon into himself. As a result, the only obstacle to his becoming Lennon was Lennon himself. At Rikers Island prison, in Hudson, he came face to face with the terrible reality that he was no more than a mere Mark David Chapman (Clarkke, 1980, p. 21)

3. Edmundo Mezger, *Criminologia,* translated by José Arturo Rodrigues Muñoz, 2nd Edition. Madrid, Editorial Revista de Derecho Privado, 1950, p. 35.

4. Gerardo Vasconcelos, *Lições de Medicina Legal,* 2nd Edition, revised and updated. Rio de Janeiro, 1976, pp. 437-438.

5. Roberto Lyra, *Direito Penal Normativo,* 2nd Edition, Rio de Janeiro, José Konfino Editor, 1977, p. 25.

Chapter 2

Tendency or Inclination towards Crime

In the complex study involving the circumstances in which Victimology points to cases where the victim can bring about or contribute towards characterization of the criminal, understanding the technical extent of the delinquent due to tendency category is of significant importance. After all, the tendency towards delinquency can be acted out as a derivation of the sentiment or sensation of concrete suffering by a victim.

The Initial Conception Regarding a Personal Tendency towards Crime

This personal tendency, in our days does not have the same orientation espoused by the Positive School during the XIX century, which defended the doctrine of the "delinquent due to congenital tendency," which, simply put, was the same thing as referring to a "natural-born delinquent." Research indicates a more remote predecessor, suggesting the classification of "criminal due to congenital tendency," the thesis presented by Enrico Ferri in *Archivo di Psichiatria* (1880, p. 474).

The Italian code of 1889 made no allusion to a criminal due to tendency. When it was being prepared, the Preliminary Project for the Penal Code for Criminal Offenses, known as the Ferri Positivist Project, spoke in article 2.1, number 3, of "abnormal organic and psychic conditions, which can reveal criminal tendencies." Article 33 also made mention of the "delinquent who, without being alienated, was in a state of chronic intoxication by alcohol or other venomous substance, or was found in a state of grave psychic anomaly." In such a situation, "the criminal should be segregated into special work colonies." This provision, however, did not apply when the psychic anomaly consisted exclusively or principally of a congenital or acquired tendency towards criminal offense.

Criminological positivism substantially favored individualizing the classification of delinquent due to congenital tendency or natural-born delinquent. Congenital tendency meant natural inclination, innate disposition towards crime, instinctive need for committing it, and, in the individual, is an abnormality of an ethical and social nature, which determines the specific manner of reaction to environmental stimuli.

In this sense, Ferri (1929, p. 189) argued that among humans, delinquent or not, in certain cases there exists a biosocial type in whom congenital or acquired characteristics prevail and lead that individual to be more or less disposed, because of his or her physio-psychical constitution, towards a certain activity or profession. Thus, there is also a purely biological or anthropological type of delinquent in whom criminal tendencies are congenital and manifest themselves from the early years on, accompanied by profound anatomical, physiognomic and also psychic characteristics, which may not be explained as having been produced in the individual solely due to life habits, nor yet by social conditions in general."

Ferri was not isolated in his studies. His doctrine received the support of renowned criminologists who at the time defended the validity of the thesis of transmission of degenerative characteristics as an effect of the laws of heredity. Garofalo (1916, p. 119) was one of those supporting "the conception that criminal tendencies and predispositions are especially transmitted by hereditary factors."

"Tendency" or "disposition" supposes a biological foundation that has large genetic potentiality. It can mean, on the one hand, a series of specific biological potentialities being developed, and, from another angle, others of the same nature that may develop. It has, furthermore, a double aspect: one side that is overt, already manifest or being manifested, and another side that is latent, which may or may not manifest itself, there being no rigid or clearly established boundary between the two zones.

The tendency is not precisely a quality or a characteristic, although it may give way to them. Nor does it consist of a clear manner of being, even though it influences the person's conduct. It is a set of active or non-active possibilities, which vary according to the complex nature of each personality and its respective dynamization in the surrounding world. Each person, even if coming from the same parents, as his or her own distinct disposition, with a negligible probability of two children being genotypically equal, since even with identical twins there is no absolute identity.

It is not a question, therefore, of conceiving of a tendency or disposition as something acquired, fixed in a definitive form for the same person, but of something variable, evolving, the consequence of a series of potentialities that make up the natural disposition, and the forces of the surrounding world that act upon them.

The external characteristics of a person may, by virtue of various interactions and joint actions, not correspond exactly to genotypical powers, given that those, because they are in principal a series of probabilities or possibilities, are capable or not of manifesting themselves completely, and, even if they manifest themselves, are subject to the configuring performance of other powers in the human constitution, or even of characteristics acquired by the body's adaptation to the surrounding world, giving rise to a result that may be different than what these characteristics might produce by themselves.

The Formation of the Judicial Structure of the Delinquent Due to Tendency

With the advent of the work of preparing the Italian Penal Code of 1930, known as the Rocco Code, a new aspect was attributed to the figure of the criminal due to tendency, as may be seen in the marked divergences between article 104 of the Preliminary Project of 1927, and the definitive wording that was adopted in article 108 of that Penal Code.

Although scholars in the field have attempted to eliminate, at different periods, doubts concerning the judicial structuring of the delinquent due to tendency, some aspects still require a more accurate analysis, since there have been countless consequences of the appearance of this classification for speculations and interpretations in the fields of Criminology, Victimology and Criminal Law.

The needs of science, which have stimulated us to establish with possible precision the convergent and divergent points of the so-called tendential delinquent, do not exclude the possibility of not being fully met in this work, since we are faced with a controversial theme, which is thus subject to the formulation of several interpretative hypothesis.

The Ministerial Report on the Definitive Project for the Italian Penal Code of 1930 made a point of leaving it clear that the provisions of article 108 of that Code had nothing to do with employment of the expression "delinquent due to instinctive tendency" adopted by the first draft of the Project.

In summary, the Ministerial Report clarified that:

> Instinctive tendency meant no more than a natural inclination, disposition towards delinquency, with its own nature; one might say an abnormality in the moral and social sense of the agent. Normality in the moral sense is a concept quite distinct from normality of intelligence and of will. The Project based itself on imputability; that is, the capacity for understanding or for desiring, but in no case does it require of the agent the consciousness of moral and social principles.

> The abnormal, as long as this does not include those with sickness of the intellect or the will, is also imputable. To avoid any doubt that might arise as to the meaning of the word 'instinctive,' the same has been eliminated from the article. (1929, t. 1, p. 156).

This was a timely clarification, because it demonstrated the exclusion of the hypotheses of total or partial defect of the mind and showed that a particular inclination for transgression could in no way be based upon diseases of the intellect or of the will.

Following up on this understanding, Manzini (1959, pp. 263-264) inserted in his treatise that the Italian Penal Code, in withdrawing the expression "delinquent due to instinctive tendency," leaving only "delinquent due to tendency," avoiding the mistake of affirming that the project wished to allude to the natural-born delinquent or any other person impelled towards transgression by psychopathological forces. Delinquents due to tendency are individuals who, despite having a lucid intellect and perfect will, lack only an ethical and social sense."

This philosophy of the Italian Code was what projected internationally the figure of the delinquent due to tendency and offered conditions for analyzing and estimating the concrete ends desired by Italian law.

The words of the Professor and Friar Gemelli (1948, pp. 311-312) express the philosophy adopted by the Italian legislators in 1930.

The divergence was not only in the text but also in the concept. The Project concerned itself with defining a type of delinquent due to instinctive tendency; in the Penal Code the special inclination towards wrongdoing in the delinquent due to tendency resides in his particularly perverse natural disposition, which is revealed in some transgressions due to the existence of a number of objective and subjective circumstances.

Faced with the arguments presented by the Positive School disciples, who affirmed that the category of tendency to transgress, adopted in the Ferri Project, represented a recognition of the doctrine that they were defending, the "Advisory Committees" responsible for the lengthy debates surrounding preparation of the Italian Code, decided to abandon the primitive formula and admit a category that would identify with the logical conclusion that some conducts existed that possessed an inclination to repeat criminal actions with some degree of ease.

This being the case, the terms of article 108 of the Italian Penal Code of 1930 thus define the tendency towards wrongdoing.

> A delinquent due to tendency shall be considered as one who, although not recidivist, habitual or professional, practices a non-negligent wrong against life or individual integrity, although not provided for in title twelve of the second book of this code, and that, singly and jointly with the circumstances indicated in the paragraph of article 133, reveals a special inclination towards wrongdoing, an inclination having origin in the particularly evil natural disposition of the guilty party. The rule of this article shall not apply if the inclination towards wrongdoing should have its origin in infirmity, as provided articles 88 and 89 of this Code.

With regard to specific treatment, according to article 109, the accentuated social risk posed by such violent delinquents induced the Italian legislature to formulate a judicial declaration on the tendency towards delinquency, with the purpose of consequently applying appropriate security measures.

The heading of criminal due to tendency in the current Italian positive Law, despite its more restricted contents, along general lines presents a biopsychical and social characterization along the same lines of the thesis previously put forth by defenders of criminological positivism. Besides the definitions found in the body of article 108, it should be noted that, while for the Positive School there were no limitations established on the concept of imputability (enshrining the principle of legal or social liability), on the contrary, for the Italian Penal Code, there is no imputability for those who lack "the capacity to understand and to desire." On the other hand, the concept of tendency adopted in the Italian

Code means that such an imputability will remain, but with a broader concept involving a certain approximation with the positivist principle of legal or social liability.

Regarding the issue, the jurist Raoul Alberto Frosali says that "article 108 does not impede an abnormality of moral consciousness from accompanying or of being a cause or an effect, in confrontation with a physio-psychic state, in which one may recognize a given infirmity that will produce a generic incapacity for understanding, wanting or of acting according to the law.

The characteristic elements of the delinquent according to tendency defined by the Italian legal document of 1930, insofar as a rational social defense are concerned, did not distance it from the category of incapacity, since the Code imposed treatment as a security measure reserved for the various categories of incapacitated persons. Article 108 does not provide for a declaration of tendency to be the result of an inclination found in incapacitated or semi-incapacitated delinquents, who are respectively dealt with in articles 88 and 89. The same reasoning is directed towards acts committed in a state of chronic intoxication produced by alcohol or stupefacient substances, as provided for in article 95 of the statute being examined." (Frosali, 1952, p. 450).

The dogmatic concept of a criminal due to tendency instituted by Italian law as revealing a notable inclination towards wrongdoing due to a particularly perverse natural disposition, was rapidly able to achieve undeniable international projection in the field of specific research and debates, which decisively contributed to the inclusion of that category in penal legislation in numerous countries.

That was one of the notable merits of Italian judicial culture; it opened doors for later scholarly work, with so many questions being raised regarding the efficacy of understanding the criminal due to tendency in the areas of Criminal law, Criminology and Victimology, exactly in opportunities provided when those Sciences directed their efforts to identifying the categories of criminal and victims susceptible to appearing and standing out in a crime scene.

Implications of the Judicial Essence of the Delinquent Due to Tendency for Criminology and for Victimology

Many specialists have inquired, with reason, as to the logical criterion for placing within Criminology (study of the delinquent) and Victimology (study of the victim) the judicial structuring of the criminal due to tendency.

We understand that the delinquent by tendency figure, provided in foreign penal legislation inspired by the Italian Penal Code, was a formulation resulting from the demand for a practical formula, although without the guarantee of scientific experimentation that would indicate such a reality existing within the natural order of things.

It is evident that, given such a legal prevision, there will always be a need for a minute and specialized study of the biopsychical formation and of the stimuli that determine antisocial conduct. Examinations of manifestations, functional personality disturbances and the perturbations of human behavior, which alter the subjective life of the individual or his or her relations in society, are fields for action for both Criminology and Victimology, and important for judgment of criminals and execution of sentences applied by Criminal Law. As a result, the close relation among the practical purposes of Criminology, Victimology and Criminal Law, legitimates the concern over the typological characteristic of the orientation followed by the legislator in classifying the delinquent due to tendency with the typical image of a crime that is horrendous, perverse or executed with a strong dose of cruelty.

We thus have two foci to consider:

1. the usual and objective manner of defining the criminal as bearing a tendency provided for in law;
2. concern over the criminological aspects of a complete analysis of the delinquent personality.

One may thus conclude, that the judicial classification of delinquent due to tendency has a double aspect: legal and criminological. Bettiol (1973, p. 33) presents the same line of thinking when stating that "it is a case of a type created by the legislator (legal type) in the presumed verification of an inclination toward crime (criminological type), so that society will be placed in a condition to prepare appropriate defense measures."

The explanation for the criminological face of structuring the delinquent due to tendency is based, as we have said, on the importance attributed to the study of personality, with a need for precisely relating individual or physio-psychic factors with the sociocultural factors inherent to evolution of human behavior in social life.

Even if one recognizes traits in disposition or internal motivation for a practical characterization of delinquency by tendency, as was expressed by Altavilla (1964, p. 384), one may never contest the powerful participation of exogenous factors, which encourage the personality to practice antisocial activities.

We bring our aptitudes, our instincts, our passions from the cradle, but moral standards are formed in the society in which we live, since the social environment impels persons in a certain direction. Thus, while giving due weight to aptitudes, instincts and passions, the criminogenous environment will always be propitious for a proliferation of delinquent behaviors.

With great pleasure, this author has ascertained that his conclusion regarding the factors that can motivate a delinquent due to tendency was the same one defended by Alessandre Lacassagne, with the only difference being that the French writer did not specifically refer to the criminal due to tendency or inclination, which was not being discussed during his time. Since the 1st International Congress on Criminal Anthropology, held in 1885 in Rome, Lacassagne, according to Casanova (1937, p. 134), had defended the supremacy of the social factor over the endogenous factor.

Human Behavior in Life of New Approaches Involving Science and Spirituality: Transpersonal Psychology, Spiritist Doctrine and Neurolinguistics

Along the vast horizon of those approaches three highly specialized domains emerge:

a. Transpersonal Psychology;
b. Spiritist Doctrine;
c. Neurolinguistics.

In the guideline related to the principle of the tendency towards delinquency, one should not the proposal of modern *Transpersonal Psychology*, which proposes to present humans as integrated and interdependent within the Universe, a foundation supported by the *Quantum Physics* Theory of Max Planck and the *Relativist Physics Theory* of Albert Einstein (Tabone, 1993, pp. 165-174).

What effectively defines the transpersonal context is the therapist's capacity for communicating, by means of attitudes, methods and psychotherapeutic techniques, the confidence necessary for helping the needy person to explore his or her transpersonal domains. This involves high personal capacity for expanding the needy person's consciousness, creating opportunities so that this person can better live on a psychological and spiritual level.

In her book *The Quantum Self,* Professor Danah Zohar, with a graduate degree in Philosophy and Religion from Harvard University, provides an interesting analysis of the *New Physics* defended by the *Quantum Physics Theory*, showing that there is a source of energy with subatomic particles that can reveal to us the physical foundation of consciousness, and, consequently, our great responsibility in the act of being, of relating with other people, of using our freedom and the extent to which use of freedom makes us responsible for our choices. Every thing and every human being will always be part of a Universe in which a system of references is introduced. In essences, says Danah Zohar "the quantum cosmovision emphasizes dynamic relationships as the basis for everything that exists. It says that our world arises by means of a mutually creative dialogue between mind and body (interior and exterior, subject and object), between the individual and his or her material and personal context, and between human culture and the world of nature. It gives us a vision of man as free and responsible, reacting to others and to the environment, essentially related and naturally committed, and, at every moment, creative." (Zohar, 1990, p. 293).

In research on the links humans have with the world of Physics, the discussion on life-death relations with the nature of the universe are equally noteworthy.

A large portion of Earth's inhabitants believe in reincarnation, supported by foundations of Religions that preach the existence of life after death. There are, in fact, fascinating accounts of people who have recorded details of a previous life, reported by Sogyal Rinpoche, according to whom everything that happens to us reflects our past Karma, and

because of this Karma—the concatenation of actions and effects introduced into the existence of a person—has a genuinely living and practical
significance in daily life, with this being the basis for Buddhist ethics.
Even if we were born in the same family, we all have different personalities, different things happen to us and we have different talents, desires
and destinies (Rinpoche, 1999, pp. 116-130).

We present below the foundations of the *Tibetan Doctrine* regarding
reincarnation and the presence of Karma supported by Sogyal Rinpoche,
one of the greatest expressions in the dialogue between Science and Spiri-
tuality.

> The West and the East have characteristic ways of escaping from the
> responsibilities that result from understanding karma. In the East, people
> use Karma as an excuse not to help anyone, saying that if they suffer it
> is due to "their Karma." In the West, with its "freedom of thought,"
> we do the opposite. Westerners who believe in Karma can be exces-
> sively "sensitive" and "careful," and say that, in fact, helping some-
> one would be to interfere in something that such a person needs to
> "work out alone." That escape is a betrayal of our humanity. It is
> perhaps equally possible that our Karma is to find a way of helping. I
> know many rich people; their wealth can be their destruction, when it
> encourages laziness and egotism, or when they waste opportunities
> money gives them to help others, and in so doing help themselves.

> We must never forget that it is by means of our actions, words and
> thoughts that we have choice. And, if we choose like that, we may put
> an end to suffering and its causes, helping our true potentialities—our
> Buddha nature—to awaken in us.

> Until our Buddhic nature is totally awakened and we are free of igno-
> rance and united with the enlightened and immortal mind, there can be
> no end to the wheel of life and death. Thus, the teachings tell us that if
> we do not assume the greatest responsibility possible for ourselves
> now, in this life, our suffering will continue not only throughout a few
> lives, but for thousands of them.

> It is this grave and serious knowledge that leads the Buddhists to af-
> firm that the future lives are even more important than the present life,
> because there are many more awaiting us in the future. That long-term
> view governs the way they lead their lives. They know that if they
> were to sacrifice all of eternity for this life, it would be like spending

the savings of an entire existence on one gulp, irresponsibly ignoring the consequences.

But if we in fact observe the law of Karma and arouse in ourselves the good heart, open towards love and compassion, if we purify our mind and step by step awaken the wisdom nature of that mind, we can become true human being, essentially enlightened. (Rinpoche, 1999, pp. 136-137).

Defenders of *Transpersonal Psychology*, the German psychologists Thorwald Dethlefsen and Rudiger Dahlke deal with describing a personality with a typical predisposition towards risks of accidents, be they in traffic, in domestic life, at work, which implies an interpretation of each occurrence based on an inner perspective of the person involved.

This is the analysis by Dethlefsen and Dahlke:

The *Law of Resonance* (cause and effect) makes it so that we never have contact with anything unrelated to ourselves. Functional correlations are always the material means necessary for a manifestation in the physical sphere. In order to paint a picture, we need canvas and paint. However, they are not the primordial cause of the painting, but the material means with whose aid the artist may give concrete form to an inner image. It would be complete foolishness to try and eliminate the interpretation of the painting with the argument that the paint, the canvas and the brush are in fact its primordial causes.

We are the ones provoking our accidents, in the same way in which we seek our illnesses. In those cases, we have no scruples in considering a given subject as if it were capable of being a cause. However, the responsibility for everything that happens in our life is ours. There is no exception to this rule; therefore, we should cease to look for one. When someone suffers, he alone is responsible for the suffering (which has nothing to do with its seriousness!). Every person is at the same time author and victim. So long as humans do not discover that they perform this dual role, it is impossible to become perfect. To the extent to which one complains about supposed external authors, we can easily see the degree of rancor that he feeds against himself as author. In this case, there is lacking an intuitive perception, that view that allows one to see that author and victim are one and the same.

The knowledge that accidents have an unconscious motivation is not new. Sigmund Freud himself suggested some time ago, in his classic

Psychopathology of Daily Life, that accidents such as slips of the tongue, forgetfulness, loss of objects and other missteps are actually the result of unconscious intentions. Since that time, psychosomatic research has been able to demonstrate—based merely on statistical data—the existence of a type of person "with a predisposition towards accidents." By this is meant a specific personality structure that tends to elaborate its conflicts in the form of accidents. Already in 1936, the German psychologist Karle Marbe described his observations in the book *Practical Psychology for Accidents in General and Traffic Accidents.* He says that a person who suffers an accident has more possibilities of suffering new accidents than those who have never been victims of them. (Dethlefsen and Dahlke, 1983, pp. 211-212)

Regarding this differentiated philosophical interpretation related to the complex human existence, Dethlefsen and Dahlke go on to say:

In his essential work on *Psychosomatic Medicine* published in 1950, Franz Alexander wrote the following notes on this theme: "In a study of traffic accidents in Connecticut it was noted that, during a period of six years, 36.4 of all accidents occurred with a small number of 3.9% of persons. A large company that hired numerous cargo truck drivers, concerned with the high cost of accidents in its fleet, sought to research their causes in an effort to reduce their frequency. Among other approaches, the also did some surveys regarding the accident history of several drivers. Those who had suffered the greatest number of accidents were placed in other jobs. This very simple measure reduced the frequency of accidents to a fifth of their original number. But the interesting result of this survey was that those drivers who had suffered a large quota of accidents, also continued having accidents in their new jobs. This irrefutably demonstrates that there is something like *persons with a predisposition towards accidents* and that they maintain that tendency regardless of the type of service in their daily lives."

Alexander also deduces that "in the majority of accidents, an intentional element is implicit, even if it can barely be consciously perceived." In other words: "the majority of accidents have an unconscious motivation, That citation from the older psychoanalytic literature has the intention of showing, among other things, that our view of accidents is not new and how lengthy the process of awareness of things (disagreeable things) is, if it really does happen after all."

For a later development of this subject, the description of a certain personality with a typical predisposition towards accidents interests us much less than the meaning of an accident in our own lives. Even when a person is not the type who has a tendency to suffer accidents, what happens in his life will have a personal significance, and we will learn to discover it. If in the life of a person one accident after another happens, this fact reveals that the person has not been able to resolve his problems in his conscience, and, therefore, is spending some time in an enforced apprenticeship. The fact that a given individual will primarily live out his corrections by means of accidents corresponds to the so-called *locus minoris resistentiae*. An accident abruptly questions the manner in which the victim does things. It is a break in his life, and as such must be analyzed. But in doing this analysis, we should not observe the general course of the accident as if it were a theater piece, trying to understand its exact structure so as to transfer it to a concrete situation. An accident is a caricature of the problem itself—and is exactly as painful and as incisive as any other caricature. (Dethlefsen and Dahlke, 1983, p. 213)

In harmony with this judgment defended by the proponents of Transpersonal Psychology, is the position of *Spiritist Doctrine*, which does not incorporate the theory of criminal heredity, although it does not reject the transmittability of morphophysiological characteristics.

In the book *Espiritismo e Criminologia*, Deolindo Amorim maintains that the inclination towards crime may be conditioned by anatomic-psychical factors. This does not mean to say that the inclination towards crime derives from those factors, since it has deeper roots and constitutes a degeneration inherent to the spirit incarnated in the personality made up of three elements: biological, environmental and spiritual.

Spiritist Doctrine does not deny then, that environmental circumstances, constitutional dispositions and the psychological deeds may be conditions favorable towards criminality, because "the spirit, being previous to the body, brings with it at incarnation, all the baggage of errors, qualities, propensities and aptitudes that may be reproduced by means of other existences." (Amorim, 1993, pp. 77-78). Thus is explained the influence of reincarnation on the origin of a crime; that is, the spirit acts as the cause of propensity towards crime and not moral or physical heredity towards crime.

A new Science directed to the study of the human accumulation of subjective experiences is *Neurolingustics*, which arose through experimental research that the Linguist Richard Blandler and the Mathematician John Grinder began disseminating in 1975 at the University of California, in the United States (Robbins, 1987, pp. 40-47).

Neurolinguistic Programming offers techniques for people to use resources that they have to their own benefit, for overcoming obstacles, maturing, being happy, making firmer decisions, and so be successful and become important points of importance and positive influence in the system where they operate within family, work and friendship circles.

Neurolinguistics allies resources from Linguistics and Neurology. Towards this end, it brings together two aspects:

a. study of the process of organizing conscious and unconscious subjective experience;
b. study of the neurological systems that form the basis of behavior, emotions, verbal and non-verbal language related to the sensory characteristics of human communication.

All of those studies lead to identification of interpersonal confrontations, where factors such as undesirable habits, guilt feelings, aggressiveness, distaste, shame, fear, phobia, insecurity and lack of self-esteem can unleash subterranean violence.

Anthony Robbin's book *Unlimited Power,* a best seller that basically deals with Neurolinguistic Programming, precisely defines the essence of the issue:

> One of the constants in life is that results are always being produced. If you do not consciously decide which results you want to produce and do not represent things in harmony with this, then some outside agent, such as a conversation, a television show, may create states that will generate behaviors that are unfavorable to you. Life is like a river. It is moving and you may be at the river's mercy, if you do not take deliberate and conscious measure to keep yourself going in the direction you have predetermined. If you do not plant the mental and physiological seeds of the results you want, weeds will undoubtedly grow. If we do not consciously guide our own minds and states, our environment may by chance produce undesirable states. The results can be disastrous. It is vital, then, for us to keep guard daily at the door of our mind, considering that we know very well how we are always acting out things to ourselves. We must pull up the weeds in our garden every day. (Robbins, 1987, p. 57)

One may add, along the same complementary line of reason, the considerations of Steve Andreas and Connirae Andreas:

> Some people are violent because they have learned that violence is an appropriate reaction in certain situations. This is an assimilated behavior. However, the majority of people become violent when they cease to have options. Think of a situation in which you were violent, or felt you were about to become violent. Was violence a *choice* among several options? Or did you feel that you had no alterative, frustrated because nothing that you had tried up till then had worked out?

> People become violent when they cease to have options and feel frustrated and impotent. When society as a whole ceases to have options for dealing with violence, it turns to repression, to control and imprisonment. This increases the feeling of impotence in the wrongdoer, which, for its part, generates more violence. The solution for the problem of violence is not more violence, but to teach other positive manners of thinking and behaving. At the individual level, learning to view others in three dimensions, obtain personal resources for feeling emotionally secure and knowing how to deal with intimacy and distance can make a great difference. (Andreas & Andreas, 1993, pp. 198-199)

The Penal Pairing and the Criminal Pairing

The effect of the initiative of being someone's accomplice based on the principle that "in union there is strength" lead the French professor Vasile Stenciu to dedicate special attention to the theories of "penal pairing" and of "criminal pairing," situations in which one may or may not identify the connection of the offender's understandings with those of the victim, which may be subject to punishment due to carrying of "associated delinquency" through complicity (Stanciu, 1985, pp. 14-16).

One should not confuse the technicality of "penal pairing," a theory originally formulated by Binyamin Mendelsohn, with the technical sense of the "criminal pairing," (criminal copying or criminality by two persons), a doctrine developed by professor Scipio Sighele, considered one of the greatest expressions in the field of Italian Criminal Law, especially because of his intellectual production and scientific foundations regarding the figure of the delinquent in the social context (Sighele, 1892, p. 9).

The "penal pairing," whose foundations are found in the biblical account of the murder of Abel by Cain,[1] is made up of an aggressor and of a victim, each one positioned at distinct or antagonistic angles, from which may arise both the completely innocent victim, as well as the victim who, through some expression of behavior, is able to profit during the course of the crime. We may cite as an example a bank robbery, in which the manager, even though under duress, takes advantage of the situation to also keep some of the stolen money.

"Criminal pairing" expresses homogenous and harmonic interests on the part of the persons acting as personages of the crime, both the author and the victim, when together, in synchronized steps, they converge and project themselves in one of the multiple ways of participating in the crime. This is the case with collusion between drug dealers and addicts, when the later, for example, steals so as to obtain money for acquiring and consuming the drug. There is a transparent synchronicity of conduct for achieving desires.

In both hypotheses—"criminal pairing" and "penal pairing"—all circumstances and details involved in the crime committed must be investigated, so that a possible judgment of reproof issued on the behavior of each agent is examined in a fair and appropriate manner.

Luíz Rodriguez Manzanera observes the possibility of a "penal pairing" being converted into a "criminal pairing," as in the probabilities of attitudes of the ruffian and the prostitute who commit infractions together. The Mexican Jurist also reminds us that the author and the victim are not always clearly opposed to each other, since there are situations where one does not find an obvious difference, as may be noted in certain cases of incest or suicide pact (Manzanera, 1988, p. 129).

In a logical analysis of the aggressor-victim link, Manzanera says that it is also important to take into account the appearance of an opportunist when tragedies appear, whom he calls the "penal third party," who can apparently pretend and present himself or herself as a witness to the situation, such as in the case of a witness to the situation, when in fact, even without connivance with the aggressor or victim, she or he skillfully takes advantage of the situation to in some fashion obtain advantage from the crime (Manzanera, 1988, p. 129). An example of this would be the person who asks for a bribe so as to protect or not denounce the aggressor or victim.

In the dynamic relation between the aggressor (author) and the victim, when considering the components of the "penal yoke" and the "criminal yoke," it is important to emphasize that the victim and the delinquent may have relations related to family, friendship, companionship or business, which is why many times the Criminal Justice system is the least appropriate venue for resolving conflicts among those persons.

Especially when the crimes involved are of low offensive power, the criminal process, instead of conciliating people, actually drives them farther apart, increasing animosity and inciting greater disdain for the rules of Law and ethics.

Punishing the one who is declared delinquent and giving satisfaction to the other who is declared the victim resolves the question in terms of the Judicial Power, but may complicate personal relations, for which reason the person of the mediator,[2] in certain occurrences, is the most suitable one for promoting rapprochement and healthy reconciliation, minimizing the disadvantages for the persons involved in the problem, while at the same time adding greater prestige to the exercise of responsible citizenship, so that the ideal that respecting the rights of others and assuming the task of human solidarity are demands of the common good will prevail.

Jean Pinatel, writing on this theme, states that criminal yoke refers to a phenomenon of identification, whose primary mechanisms are *introspection* (placing the other within oneself) and *projection* (placing oneself in the other). This phenomenon of identification may be observed, in another conjuncture. In the *Hegelian* dialectic of *master-slave*, in which the slave, who must offer to the master the fruit of work on which he or she almost totally depends, harbors with regard to the latter a feeling of hatred that can be manifested both in desiring the death of the master or of his or her own death. This is the stereotype of a situation that may be accepted as submission, with the development of an inferiority complex and also a feeling of culpability, with regard to what may be considered the factors that influence somatic constitution, that are reflected in the psyche, and, consequently, in motivation for crime.

Among these factors are not only those of whom the person is conscious, but also unconscious factors which, even when they do not transcend the threshold of consciousness, enter the psychic workings and influence deliberation of motives and the decision to transgress. This dialectic designs both the mechanism of collection, mass reactions, and interpersonal phenomena. One may see, for example, that the psychology of behavior of colonized peoples, based on manifestations of collective dependency, directed by a sentiment of inferiority or culpability, may be impelled towards revolt driven by violence aggressiveness. In a similar situation, one frequently sees, the path followed by "criminal pairing" being transformed into "penal pairing," that is, the mutation of "criminality by two" into "criminality directed by only one of two *partnenaires,*" an occurrence that Pinatel calls "crime of freeing." (Pinatel, 1961, p. 342).

The dangerousness of the "criminal pairing" was studied by Sighele, who developed research on the theme (Pinatel, 1961, p. 343). Sighele believed that the succubus (subordinated, commanded, directed) has the potential for "positive dangerousness," resulting from its disposition to do evil spontaneously, as well as having "negative dangerousness," resulting from its being willing to do evil by suggestion or dependence. Pinatel does not think that way. For him, the psychological cause of wrongdoing by the *succubus* consists in the persistent, energetic action of the *incubus* (subordinator, commander, director), who acts and persists to such an extent that it overcomes all resistance by the commanded (*non agit sed agitur*). Even though it originates from weak dangerousness, action by the succubus cannot exist without intervention by the dominant character. Taking into account the positions of Sighele and Pinatel, we believe that the problem of dangerousness of the victims, which are involved in the "criminal pairing" is closely linked to the conception of victim due to tendency, a topic we have dealt with previously.

The study of interpersonal relations in the "criminal pairing" and the "penal pairing" leads us to conclude that, in one situation or the other, rarely will one find absolute opposition between the delinquent and the victim; among other reasons, because frequently there is reciprocal action. In some cases it is chance that will determine who will be which, as occurs in the case of a duel, where both contenders have the same intention of using their weapons more rapidly to fight their rivals. Luck and skill will determine who will become the victim.

Another aspect to consider is the question raised by Lewis Lawes, quoted by Cornil, when he refers to the reality of "who is whom" in relations that are established in the paradigms of "criminal yoke" and of "penal yoke." (Cornil, 1959, p. 598). Knowing "who is whom," in various sex infractions can lead, for example, to determining the mechanism for the victim's adhesion, as can be seen in the formalization of conduct selected by the prostitute and by the pimp, who exploits the prostitute.

As possible projections of the author and the victim to allow identification of the "penal yoke" or "criminal yoke," Versele puts forth three types of relations: a) *neurotic relation;* b) *psychological relation;* c) *genobiological relation.* It should be noted that these three relationship mechanisms can also act in combination. (Versele, 1962, pp. 593-595).

The *neurotic relation* is capable of arising through a precocious disturbance in the affective limits that link a person to his or her parents. An accentuated link of dependence and respect for the father, accompanied by a marked *Oedipal* tendency (Oedipus complex) towards the mother, may provide favorable terrain for converting the person into a victim.

The *psychological* relation has to do with the reciprocal attraction between the author and the victim, through their component structures, always in search of behavioral complementarity. That is what happens with the masochist engaging with his or her partner's sadistic tendencies, and it can also occur in relations involving a swindler and a dishonest victim who makes use of the swindle or trick to also obtain some sort of advantage.

The *genobiological relation* is founded on an attraction derived from a similar hereditary makeup. This attraction, according to Versele, was demonstrated through genealogical research carried out by L. Rittler in Germany in 1937, when he discovered the ways in which a certain number of vagrants, beggars and thieves were as if attracted one to the other, independently of their social and economic living standards in the community.

Jean Penatel classified these three modalities of interpersonal relations into three types of victims: *determinant victim, facilitating victim* and *socializable victim.*

In the neurotic relation one finds the *determinant victim*, who causes, with his or her personality disturbance, disastrous acts to her or himself.

In the psychological relation the *facilitating victim* appears, who arouses the author's appetite (*la victime éveille l'apetit*) by bringing about the occasion for a criminal act, as can be seen in blackmail or in swindling practices, when the delinquent plays with the victim's dishonest instinct, which may be manifesting an unconscious desire to allow himself or herself to be harmed, due to feeling attracted by the desire for easy profit or illicit advantage.

In the genobiological relation the possibility arises of applying the principles and rules of Pedagogy, Psychology and Psychiatry to reorient the *socializable victim*, in conditions of obtaining social readaptation for him or herself and moral elevation for the community.

Questions involving the victim's personality, biological and moral features, environmental diversities, socio-criminal mutations, the possible correlation with the criminal, as well as the connection of the victimological role that may be in play in the genesis of the crime. All of these have been the objects of contemplation in successive studies and research, not only because of scientific implications, but because of concerns related to the correct application of judicial organization in the interaction of values in society, which favors healthy exercise of citizenship.

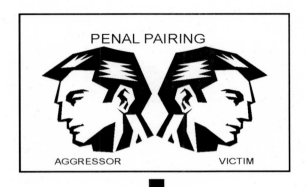

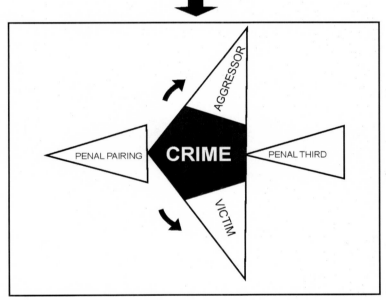

PENAL PAIRING

Aggressor and victim, position themselves at distinct or antagonistic angles, even though the victim may gain advantage from the crime. Example: in a Bank robbery, the Manager, even though under duress, takes advantage of the situation to also keep some of the stolen money.

PENAL THIRD PARTY

One who, even without connivance with the aggressor or victim, seeks in some fashion to obtain advantage from the crime. Example: person who asks for a bribe so as to protect or not denounce the aggressor or victim.

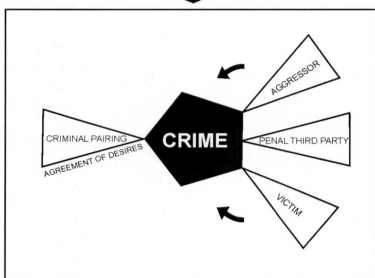

CRIMINAL YOKE

Synchronism of conduct due to agreement of desires. The aggressor and the victim, in synchronized steps, reveal homogenous and harmonic interests in the relations that converge towards crime. Example: "criminality by two" practiced by the drug dealer in collusion with the addict.

PENAL THIRD PARTY

One who, even without connivance with the aggressor or victim, seeks in some fashion to obtain advantage from the crime. Example: person who asks for a bribe so as to protect or not denounce the aggressor or victim.

Notes

1. According to the Bible, Cain killed Abel and thus, Abel went down in History as the first human victim on Earth, in a pioneering case of "penal yoke." Abel was the example of submissive victim, eliminated by the action of rebellious human nature represented by Cain.

2. Two institutions provide the advantage of swifter and more equitable administration of Justice in harmony with the modern vocation of Criminal Law, which is to punish only that which really exceeds the bounds of tolerability: a) the institution of *diversion* or *dejudicialization;* b) the institution of *mediation.*

Diversion or *dejudicialization* should be understood as the form of resolving a human conflict that has the nature of a judicial-criminal problem, bringing about pacification or reconciliation of the infractor with the victim, without the use of normal Criminal Justice proceedings. Thus, situations of conflict that can be solved before a guilty verdict or determination of a sentence should be considered as *diversion* or *dejudicialization.*

Mediation, on the other hand, while not essentially diverging from *diversion,* has one specificity. *Mediation* operates outside of judicial processes and is carried out through what we might call "intervention of a mediator," that is, a third party who enters the conflict to perform the social role of suggesting or establishing new bridges of communication, rapprochement and reconciliation between the parties. The mediator should maximize the utility of the most favorable situation and minimize the disadvantage of the most unfavorable situation.

Chapter 3

The Study of Personality

Before dealing with aspects of the victim's dangerousness, we shall present an overview of scientific knowledge related to the study of personality and its components of individuality known as **temperament** and **character.** Those components are priceless, exactly because from their bases may arise the imbalance in conduct that will occur with any possible hypothesis of precipitation towards crime involving the varieties of the victimological phenomenon.

Background

The ancient world knew the idea of *person* but not that of *personality*, which is an essential attribute of personality. The word **personality** itself did not exist in classical Latin; it appeared during the medieval period to indicate a complex of predicaments. Exactly because it designates a system, an organization, the word "personality" seems to vary in content whenever one thinker overestimates one of the ingredients of a person's makeup. Using a simile from Physics, one might say that personality is the result of a composition of forces. Or, availing ourselves of a comparison with what occurs in the domain of Chemistry, we would say that it is a compound, in which the elements do not mix but interpenetrate to form a new body.

Personality is, therefore, a synthesis, although for the purposes of study it may be the object of analysis by sectors. Nonetheless, one must take care not to forget that this disassociation into component parts is done on the epistemological and not the ontological plane. In other words, decomposition is done for the purposes of study and learning, but the personality in itself remains one single thing.

Aristotle, even without reaching the concept of personality, provided the elements that would lead medieval philosophers to develop it. His thinking regarding the person evolved and was perfected. In the first phase, faithful to his master Plato, Aristotle defended the existence of two distinct and opposing substances: body and soul. These would unite in an *accidental* and *transitory manner*. In a second stage in his thinking, Aristotle began to conceive of hylomorphism, that is, the body as an instrument of the soul. The latter acts in it and directs it as a well-governed city. Body and soul, although distinct, make up a unique compound that gives rise to all human actions. Those may not be attributed separately or exclusively to the body or to the soul, but to the subject that results from the union of both. Aristotle himself used a simile to explain his thought: "Just as the eye encompasses the pupil and sight, thus do body and soul together form man." (Fraile, 1971, pp. 498-490).

The medieval philosophers, beginning with the Aristotelian teaching that the soul is the source of all human activity and that the way a person behaves depends on the dispositions of both the soul and the body, "found, in the XIII century, the key to relations between the bodily and the psychic phenomena." (Codon & Saiz, 1968, vol. 1, p. 43). Thus, they achieved a unitary and substantial psychophysical conception of personality. That was to be the mode of *being-human* of each person. The French existentialists, from Gabriel Marcel forward, reached a quite similar conclusion, when they affirmed that "the individual *has* and the person *is*." (Geiwitz, 1973, pp. 56-58). In other words, a human being, as an individual, is passive and *has* a given nature; however, as a person, he or she *is* active, and takes a given form that distinguishes her or himself from any other individual. One may theoretically conceive of the existence of two identical diamonds, but there can be no two identical persons, because each has a unique personality.

Concept of Personality

Modern psychologists and philosophers have sought to define, or at least to conceptualize personality. Before attempting to reach a definition, however, it would be useful to make clear in what sense the word is employed, to avoid the penalty of falling into a labyrinth of verbal confusions.

The term *personality* designates, in common language, the more or less agreeable *appearance* of someone. When, for example that a house has more personality than a pair of overalls or that a certain theater actor has lots of personality, the term is being used with a meaning very different to that attributed to it by Psychology. Personality, in the popular sense, designates the *external* effect one caused by someone on other people.

In Psychology, on the other hand, personality refers to someone's internal structure. It may be considered the result of several somatic and psychic components that assure each person his or her own identity in time and space. In time, it gives unity, permanency and constancy. In space, it differentiates her or him from any other person.

The concept of personality, in Psychology, is purely ontological, referring to the thing in itself, with no value judgment (Barbe, 1915, p. 146). The genius and the dunce, the saint and the delinquent, the hero and the coward, each has a personality.

Alongside this understanding, as has been well pointed out by Álvaro Cabral and Eva Nick, there is an axiological concept into which a value element comes in. There would thus be good and bad personalities (Cabral & Nick, 1974, p. 304). Personality transcends the field of Psychology and enters that of Ethics. This is the sense in which the term is employed in the current Brazilian *Penal Code*, when referring to the length of the sentence (article 59), probation (article 77), verification of dangerousness (article 97) and so on. Naturally, this ethical concept of personality involves psychology and adds a value judgment element to it.

Some authors hold that we do not know the personality in itself, but only the operations, acts, actions and reactions of each person. Others reach the point of affirming that there is no certainty as to the limits of the existence of personality and we should thus not use a single concept, but work only with the categories of *stimulus* and *response* (Skinner, 1938, p. 305). The truth is that no instrument or conclusive assessment can reach the extreme of denying the existence of the personality. No one would say that the dark side of the moon does not exist simply because we do not see it.

Constitution of the Personality

In the human body the organs are gathered into systems according to their common function (respiratory system, digestive system, circulatory system). In the spirit the faculties are exercised according to their purpose (reason, will, sentiment). Body and soul act, with the *action* of each one reflecting on the other and provoking a joint *reaction*. The two are closely linked. They interpenetrate and form a single organization (a *compositum,* to use the terminology of medieval doctors). It is commonly said that the personality is the psychophysical organization of each person, who knows him or herself, decides things, adapts to the environment and adapts the environment to her or himself, seeking to dominate nature and place it at his or her service. Gordon Willard Allport has a very similar concept: "Personality is the dynamic organization, in the individual, of psychophysical systems that determine his behavior and his characteristic thoughts." That definition, however, does not make it clear if the person determines him or herself freely or is determined by psychic and physiological factors. And, on the other hand, it does not accentuate the person's action on the environment.

Physical and psychic factors interpenetrate, act and react reciprocally in forming the personality. The connection between physical and psychic is such that a physical impulse is not only the body responding, and is not only the mind that responds to a psychic stimulus, since in both cases it is the entire person.

Other studies have expanded on the specificities of this theme.

José Cabanis, in his work *Du Rapport du Physique et du Moral de l'Homme*, sought to reduce all psychic activity to the physiological field. Thought, sentiment, emotions, instincts, habits, all would be the pure and simple result of bodily organs (Cabanis, 1802, p. 57). In other words, he suppressed the problem of physical and psychic relations instead of resolving it.

For his part, René Descarte, although admitting the existence of two sources of energy, soul and body, maintained that they act in parallel, and do not meet, much less interpenetrate (França, 1943, pp. 221-224). Modern Psychology has reached conclusions based on observation and experience that are quite different from those achieved by the two illustrious French thinkers, whom we have mentioned.

Professor Anne Anastasi adds that in the current state, "the psychologist responds in a manner very similar to that of the hematologist responsible for examining a patient's blood, be it in analyzing the intellectual level, special activities and results and personality tests in general." (Anastasi, 1980, p. 21).

One should also note that diseases of the body do not always contribute towards *forming* the personality. But they may *deform* it. They may not be efficient causes but can be deficient causes. They may perturb, alter and even annihilate the personality.

They are like the bomb that does not build a building but can destroy it. One need only remember what happens to someone submitted to brainwashing and what happens to those addicted to psychotropic drugs, which produce depersonalizing shocks that modify character (Palmieri, 1964, vol. 2, pp. 586-587). Regarding the psychotropic drugs, we shall return to them in the Chapter dealing with personality disturbances associated to the victim's dangerousness.

Influence of Physical Factors on Psychism

It is certain, observed and even verified in the laboratory, that the vibration of sensory nerves causes the phenomena of sensation and external perception. Exogenous factors, such as climate, air that is breathed and food influence a person's temperament, character, tastes, capacity, aptitudes and greater or lesser control over passions.

Temperament depends very much on internal secreting glands, or, more correctly, on segregated hormones. Daily observation shows that some chronic illnesses, such as dyspepsia and anemia, lead to sadness, laziness and susceptibility. Contrariwise, ease of digestion brings good humor. A clear and beautiful day makes us happy and, in the Romance languages, people say "everything is blue," is well (*nel blu dipinto di blu,* in the Italian song). A sky loaded with dark clouds also darkens the soul and thus people become taciturn and despondent. It is a clearly seen and proven fact that the expression on one's face conditions the state of the soul and vice-versa. The popular saying is right that says "one who sings chases away evils."

The influence of the physical on the psychic is easily noted when we observe our own animic reactions to external factors. Heat, cold, light, darkness, an insect bite, a burn, all produce typically psychic phenomena. We may take as an example an organic lesion produced in a person by fire. It starts with the human body coming in contact with something hot. This brings about an alteration in the tissues, a purely *physical* phenomenon that would equally occur with an inanimate body. That is the *impression;* the mark from the heat remains imprinted on the body.

Since humans are not inanimate, the impression determines in them an impression that is no longer purely physical, but *physiological: innervation*. Sensitive nerves carry to the brain news of the shock and the person becomes conscious of the organic problem; it is a psychological problem, which consummates the sensation of burning.

Analysis of the phenomenon would be identical if we were to take as an example any other impression: obtained through taste, sight, smell, touch or hearing.

Influence of Psychic Factors on the Physical State

Everyone knows, through personal experience, that after having seen a figure, heard a sound, felt a pain, one may then imagine, may represent to one's inner self, the figure no longer seen, the sound no longer heard, the pain no longer felt. "The image is the projection on the psychic screen of sensible phenomena" (Janet, 1944, p. 149). It is naturally less clear in is content and more imprecise in its contours, than the original sensation. Sometimes it is even stripped of some agreeable or disagreeable tonalities. This explains why a painful fact or a complicated phase of life may be later imagined without suffering or even with sweet nostalgia.

The perception of a phenomenon and the sensation someone feels are directly linked to reality and impose themselves in overwhelming fashion on the spirit. The image that is formed of them, to the contrary, only proposes itself, offers itself, does not impose itself. All of this allows the normal, hygid, healthy person to distinguish between a perception or sensation, on the one hand, and a simple image on the other.

It is obvious that present sensations reduce the strength of images from past facts. That is why Hipólito Taine[1] called those present sensations *image reducers* (França, 1943, p. 300), even though past facts maintain a certain representative efficacy, which is affective and even a driving force. I contemplate Notre Dame Cathedral and can thereafter "see it" with my eyes closed; in other words, I can imagine it. I hear Handel's "Hallelujah Chorus," and can mentally reproduce it as many times as I wish.

An imagination does not influence only the cognitive life. It goes farther, since the images cause joy, pleasure, pain, anguish. Continuing with its action, the image acts on the nervous system, with reflexes on the sensory and motor organs. When I imagine a labial sound, the lips tend to move closer; when I imagine a horizontal movement the eyes move from right to left (or vice-versa); if I imagine a vertical movement they move up and down (or in the opposite direction).

The strength of such an image is the reason for phenomena such as sympathy, mimicry, empathy and suggestion. This image power is what Alfredo Fouillé called "idea-force" (Mora, 1941, p. 212). It has important reflexes in the field of ethics, since it explains the possibility of self-determination through which humans conduct their actions with will and intelligence.

When one admits the reality of the idea-force, the strength of images, one reaches important conclusions:

- an image can unleash action;
- the action begun tends to be consummated;
- the image can have its efficacy neutralized by perceptions, sensations or sentiments that are contrary to it.

If *nothing* opposes itself to the course of imagination, it can become translated into activity, as is the case with a sleepwalker or someone hypnotized. Thus, humans can think and act based on images. If they influence the body, ideas do so as well.

The influence of the will over the body is easily perceptible with voluntary movement. I want to stand and I stand. I want to write and I do. If, by means of sensitive nerves, the physical realm acts on the psychic realm, by means of motor nerves the psychic acts on the physical.

The analysis of what happens in the latter shows that the same phases described above regarding the influence of physical over psychic realms occur, but in reverse order. The starting point is the will, a psychic phenomenon: *I want* to walk and I walk. The action of the soul is transmitted to the body by *innervation*, that is, through unleashing activity of the efferent, motor nerves—a physiological phenomenon—which will move the muscles. How the synapse[2] operates is a mystery that science has yet to unravel (Fortes & Pacheco, p. 1011). Will it do so one day? God only knows. One thing, however, is certain. I want to walk and I walk. I want to write and I write. I want to thank God and I do so.

An approximate simile for what happens is that of an electric current transmitted through a wire. But one must bear in mind that the comparison is not entirely exact: "nervous impulses are transmitted much more slowly: from 100 to 150 meters per second, which explains why the body sometimes is slow to react." (Schiferes, 1964, p. 310).

Another reasonable comparison is that of the nervous ganglions, the associative nerve cells (of which the brain is made up) and a telephone switchboard. But it is evident that brain function is infinitely more complex and mysterious. The association neurons allow the body to interpret the sensations and transform them into orders, which are transmitted by the motor nerves.

The influence of the psychic over the physical, as attested to by Robert Lundin, is easily noticed in the violent reactions that certain strong *emotions* cause in the body: paleness, quickened pulse, perspiration, trembling, syncope, fear, hatred, jealousy, rage, sadness, etc. (Lundin, 1977, p. 330). All of the physiological functions may be affected: digestion slows down, breathing becomes panting, circulation speeds up, and secretions greatly increase. The effects of *passion* on the body are even more visible, profound and lasting. Michel Montaigne was right when he affirmed that "more men die because of the spirit than because of the body." And thus, as it kills, the spirit also saves. Confidence, the desire to live, spiritual energy all help to heal the body. And the opposite also happens, as fear, desire for death, discouragement all contribute towards aggravating organic ills[3] in our world (Lahr, 1926, p. 216).

The Temperament

Temperament is the physical disposition of each person for reacting to emotional stimuli. It has a close correlation with the body's metabolic and chemical alterations, especially those carried out in the endocrine glands.

Physical environment agents (climate, altitude, nature of the soil, rainfall regime, the air we breathe, etc.) or personal agents (somatic constitution and organic functioning) influence each person's temperament.

Everyone is born with a given temperament. It was formerly said that one died with it, that is, that temperament did not vary. Today it is said that temperament changes with age, with the type of life, with climate and so on (Allport, 1974, p. 58). Despite this, one recognizes that it is easier to change habits than temperament. Allport reminds us that "temperament may change during development of the personality. However, it continues to be true that in our makeup, beginning at birth, there are constitutional, chemical, metabolic and neural levels that establish, for us, characteristic resources. Change is possible, but not unlimited."

Hippocrates, in the fifth century before the Common Era, taught that there were four types of temperament, according to the predominance of one of four humors: the *phlegmatic* temperament (in which phlegm predominates: lymph, sera, nasal mucous, intestinal mucus, saliva); the *sanguine* temperament (in which blood predominates); the *choleric* temperament (superiority of yellow bile) and the *melancholic* temperament (predominance of black bile or *atra bilis*). Claudius Galenus maintained that the latter led to irritability and hypochondria.

Without discussing the correctness of this conception, we may note that it was followed by the philosophers: Plato (*Timeus,* 86-B in the Burnet edition, Oxford, 1899-1906), Aristotle (*Physicorum libri*, VIII, in the Ross edition, Oxford, 1950), Seneca (*De Ira,* II, 18, Beltrani edition, Oxford, 1931), and Lucretius (*De natura rerum,* 288, Bailey edition, Oxfor, 1947).

Likewise, during the medieval period the Theory of Humors was supported especially by Avicenna and Averroes, a period marked by the decline of Hippocratic teaching and support for the existence of three types of temperament, according to the predominance of sulfas, salt or mercury (Diamond, 1957, pp. 126-127).

Among the moderns, Wilhelm Wundt returned to Hippocrates' thinking with his "Physiological Psychology." Hoffding, Kulpe, Ebbinghaus, Klages and even Pavlov also admitted a quadripartite classification based upon humors (Wundt, 1952, vol. 2, p. 159). This is explained by the fact that it begins with a reality: the body's chemistry. And it is open to several interpretations.

But we should not forget that, in this area, every typology represents only a static scheme, while humans are dynamic beings: someone who is phlegmatic may at times have a choleric explosion; a sanguine person has moments of melancholy. There was a well-known case of a Catalan terrorist who coldly murdered people and yet took pleasure in petting animals.

Current studies in Endocrinology indicate that the temperament is a function not only of internal secretory glands, but of the entire body of each person, both in constitution and physiology, so much so that the study or temperament today is given the name Constitutional Psychology. We may say that John "is good-natured," to indicate a pleasant temperament, that Joseph "has a bad temper," to attribute a bitter temper to him, that Mary is docile and pleasant, to mean that she has a calm, tranquil and balanced temperament.

On the other hand, psychologists have been using the tactic of measuring and assessing temperaments by using tests. They employ the standards of *impulse* and *vigor* on the one hand and *apathy* on the other. An intense metabolism and proper functioning of the thyroid gland lead to a vigorous and impulsive temperament. A lower rhythm of metabolism and a lazier thyroid are conducive to indolence and indifference.

Character

The lexicons explain that the word **character** arose from the Greek "charakter" and means **mark, sign, badge, figure, type.**

But the word **character** is employed in two different senses. In the first, it means the manner of being of each person; every person has a character. In the second, with an ethical content, it indicates someone's firmness and correctness. With this meaning we say that a person has a good character, a bad character, or is lacking in character.

In any case, the character is the person's own nature. It is the set of qualities that identifies someone, it is the way the person feels, thinks, acts and reacts.

Each person inherits a given *disposition* (inclinations, tendencies), is born with it. The disposition contains the original temperament and character, which philosophers and psychologist call *natural*, but which could perhaps be better designated as *"the nature" of each one*. As with the physiognomy, this "natural " changes over time, but still maintains its force of reaction. Of it one can repeat the saying" of Horatius: "Expel nature with blows of a pitchfork and it will return" (*"Naturam expelles furca, tamen usque recurret,"* Horatius, 1950, vol. 2, p. 186).

It is known that if one cuts the trunk of a pine tree, one branch will bend upward and vertically follow the course of the severed part. That is also the way of human nature. A good person, who is struggling to extirpate evil dispositions, knows how easy it is to fall back into the "natural," to return to the temperament and the character one brings from the cradle.

This does not mean, however, that character cannot be changed; it may be weakened or strengthened. To the original inherited character are added acquired characters, which can either deform or reform it. That is the foundation of education. Plato correctly observes that "the good man, a lover of order and harmony, who is lapidated throughout his lifetime, is a jeweler, whose masterpiece is himself." (Lahr, 1926, vol. 1, p. 170). It is not easy forming one's own character. It is each person's struggle against him or herself, against the defects of one's "natural." This struggle requires goodwill, perseverance, and, above all, patience in the one doing the struggle. In this struggle one must not be demanding or wish to morally enrich oneself all at once. Thomas à Kempis was right: "If each year we were to eradicate one fault, we would not take long to become perfect." (*"Si omni anno unum vitium extirparemus, cito viri perfecti efficieremur,"* Kempis, 1970, p. 25).

Just as saving leads to wealth, also perseverance in correcting defects leads to perfection. Virtue is nothing more than the habit of doing good, and habit is a second nature. Successive capitulations of the will to evil end in depravity; one loses self-control and becomes a slave to vice. In contrast, small victories in the struggle against evil inclinations strengthen the character and one becomes master of oneself. Good people are athletes of the spirit who are constantly exercising.

That being the case, one who understands that formation of character brings in itself the characteristics of life itself will not be in error.

> From a seed grows an ear of corn; from the meeting of male and female cells is born a human being. In the same way, character formation is also the goal of a process of human integration. To professor Wilhelm Arnold the "idea of perfection in every being (the essence of Aristotle's "entelechial principle") clearly shows how much the structure of character is intrinsically linked to the development of the person as a whole." (Arnold, 1975, p. 40)

Notes

1. For Taine, universal ideas do not exist. Knowledge is a "true hallucination." The "self" is no more than a chain of states of consciousness, a "polyper of images." "Virtue and vice are products of nature like sugar and vitriol." A human is reduced to "an animal of a higher species who produces philosophies and poems more or less as silkworms produce their cocoons and bees their hives."

2. Synapse (from the Greek SYN, a prefix meaning to join) is the communications point between the neurons, that is, the region where the nervous impulse is transmitted from one neuron to the other.

3. Charles Lahr illustrates this with a curious episode from an Oriental legend. The angel of death appeared to a sultan to announce that his subjects

would be struck by the plague. "How may will die?" the sultan asked. "Six thousand," the angel answered. It so happened that twenty-four thousand died, and thus, the sultan observed "Thou has deceived me. Four times as many than thou didst prophecy have died." The angel responded, "Not so, six thousand died of the plague. The others, of fear."

Chapter 4

Personality Disturbances Associated to Dangerousness of the Victim

The major topical benefit that we will now examine lies in verifying the probable identity existing between the victim who precipitates occurrence of the crime and a given type of personality affected by some psychic perturbation. Above all, this happens due to perturbations which, instead of being clearly revealed, conceal themselves behind the most varied organic elements, contributing to the individual infractor being able to situate his or her behavior within some degree of full legal capacity or extenuated legal capacity.

From the medical-legal point of view, the single paragraph in article 26 of the Penal Code refers exactly to persons having perturbed mental health, even if those disorders may not constitute mental illness. It has become the practice to call individuals afflicted by such disturbances "semi-responsible," persons who, because of their relative capacity for understanding the illicit nature of the fact they have practiced or of determining themselves according to this understanding, have their legal capacity mitigated and are placed on an intermediate scale between the sane of mind and the completely insane.

The reduction of legal capacity means a reduction of culpability. If the person has a lower capacity for resisting impulses; that is, if he or she succumbs to a given criminal stimulus, the liability will be less and the degree of culpability less intense (Maurach, 1962, pp. 120-121). That being the case, whoever fits such a category will not be fully responsible, nor entirely imputable; for which reason if the Criminal Court Judge decides that the defendant is relatively liable, the Judge must mitigate the penalty resulting from the conviction.

Personality disturbances, according to the teachings of Alfred Freedman, Harold Kaplan and Benjamin Sadock (1975, pp. 73-91) encompass the following configurations:

a. psychopathic personalities;
b. sexual deviancies;
c. alcoholism;
d. drug dependence.

Psychopathic Personalities

These are disturbances characterized by lists of unadapted conducts, which are profoundly implanted, generally over a long period in the patient's life, with these anomalies being identified during adolescence and even during childhood.

The concept of psychopathic personality many times is employed with the same broad meaning of abnormal personalities in general. To avoid certain confusions, Kurt Schneider, a famous professor at Heidelberg University in Germany, known as one of the greatest authorities in the study of psychopathic personalities, advises against mixing the examination of concrete cases of those diseases with analysis of other types of abnormalities, exactly because psychopaths are individuals who, despite generally having an average or high intellectual level, externalize conduct disturbances of an ethical or anti-social nature, with difficulties in learning norms for sociability and common sense (Schneider, 1976, p. 43).

One should also establish that abnormality does not have a broad meaning of disease. Schneider (1976, pp. 29-30) teaches that "the concept of infirmity, principally in Psychiatry, in its proper sense, exists only at the somatic level, and we should only call psychic anomalies "morbid," when they may be traced to morbid organic processes. Applying "morbid" to psychic or purely social manifestations, without this basis, is merely an image, and does not have any scientific value."

Since the nineteenth century, specialists have been seeking to unveil the possible causes of psychopathic deviancies. Differing opinions still exist today, between those who teach that these deviancies originate with a certain constitutional predisposition, those who claim to find the origin in functional deficiencies in the brain, and those who believe that they can define the cause for deviancies in the possible rejection suffered by the child during the first years of life. What researchers do agree on is in recognizing that the syndrome for psychopathic personalities is distinct from deficiencies related to psychosis and neurosis, although there is a marked similarity between psychopathy and other neurotic disturbances and certain modalities of psychosis, given that, in the final analysis, neurotics, psychotics and psychopaths are unadapted personalities.

With regard to the possibility of recuperating psychopaths, Langelüddeke (1072, pp. 508-509) considers that treatment for those individuals is "not a very gratifying task, because it has not been easy for medical science to make psychopathy susceptible to cure." As was also noted by Delgado (1966, p. 132), "childhood is the most appropriate period for combating such anomalies, especially because, in that phase, treatment has the positive influence of environmental factors that stimulate good character formation."

Of the various typologies of psychopathic personalities, the one proposed by Schneider (1936, p. 38) has been the one most accepted among specialists in the field. This is undoubtedly due to precision of its categorization and the comprehensive list of all ten groups, well structured and with precise differences.

The groups defined by Schneider are the following: hyperthymic, depressive, insecure, fanatical, ostentatious, inconstant, explosive, insensitive, abulic and asthenic. The asthenic psychopaths are placed in three subgroups: sensitive asthenics, persons with a feeling of incapacity and persons easily subject to disturbances of their organic functions.

Schneider did not forget to emphasize the possible combination of features of different types, as well as the possibility of signs appearing in individuals who declaredly possessed normal personalities. He also recommended "not to confuse the determination of a type with a medical diagnosis. In diagnosis, we work with nosographic entities, concepts that are perfectly delimited and defined. The types, in contrast, are merely schematisized patterns, by which we may measure them and compare them. In diagnosis we affirm that an individual has or does not have a certain disease. In classifying a type, the affirmation cannot be so peremptory and we limit ourselves to verifying that an individual comes more or less close to this or that type." 1936, p. 38).

One cannot deny the real validity of the statement above, for when we say, for example, that a certain individual is despotic, we are not employing that designation as a diagnosis. It is not reasonable to draw a line between the despotic and other individuals, a line that will absolutely separate them. There are individuals who completely correspond to the despotic type we imagine, while others only do so approximately and still others present only a few characteristics.

The ten types that we have just cited are found combined in different manners. There are frequent combinations of fanatic explosives, depressed insecure, asthenic abulics and hyperthymic insensitives, with characteristics of the ostentatious types. Other combinations, however, will never be encountered. It is impossible to presume, Schneider affirms (1936, p. 52) that "someone insecure is at the same time insensitive."

One should also make note, in light of the lessons taught by Schneider, of the viability of frequent combinations of psychopathic personalities with the different degrees of mental debility, as is the case of the hyperthymic who is mentally deficient and has characteristics of an insensitive individual. Except for the insecure, who are almost always intelligent individuals, all of the other psychopathic personalities can be accompanied by mental deficiency.

All evidence indicates that psychiatry still has difficulties in identifying the relations between psychopathic personalities and psychoses, a situation that generates serious doctrinal controversies involving the complete study of psychopathic problems. Knowing whether we should consider certain hyperthymic and depressive types as permanent cases of cyclothymia (manic-depressive madness); seek to establish relations uniting inconstant types to epilepsy and cyclothymia; locate the relations of certain fanatics and certain insensitives with schizophrenia are only a few of the many problems involved in this complex area of medical science.

How many and what are the types of psychopathic personalities is another aspect where we cannot establish precise numbers. The ten groups produced by Schneider have been tested and today are almost unanimously accepted by other scholars in the field, but in no passage of his work did he assert that he had exhausted the possible hypotheses and other factors related to characterizing and prognosticating psychopathic symptoms.

To complement this discussion, some of the forms of expression for psychopathic personalities recognized by modern psychiatry are presented as follows (Schneider, 1987):

   a. *paranoid personality*—conduct characterized by unjustified
      suspicion, hypersensitivity, jealousy, envy, rigidity, exces-
      sive importance of the *ego* and a tendency to blame and at-

tribute evil intentions to the others, symptoms that frequently interfere with the capacity to maintain satisfactory interpersonal relations;

b. *cyclothymic personality*—conduct marked by emotional states with alternating and recidivating periods of euphoria, optimism, ambition, great energy and enthusiasm, or depression, pessimism, little energy, worry and a feeling of futility;

c. *schizoid personality*—conduct marked by reserve, hypersensitivity, isolation, fleeing from intimate relations, competitiveness, eccentricity, hostility or aggression;

d. *explosive personality*—conduct marked by sudden bursts of aggressiveness or rage, that are notably different from the patient's normal conduct;

e. *obsessive-compulsive personality*—conduct marked by an excessive concern with conformity and rigid rules of conscience. The patient may be inflexible, excessively scrupulous, excessively submissive, very inhibited and incapable of getting away from a fixed idea.

f. *hysterical personality*—conduct marked by emotional instability, excitability, hyperactivity, vanity, immaturity, dependence and dramatization of the self, a personality that tries to attract attention and be seductive;

g. *asthenic pesonality*—conduct marked by little energy, easy fatigability, lack of enthusiasm, incapacity for enjoying life and hypersensitivity to stress;

h. *antisocial personality*—conduct that encompasses non-socialized persons who are in conflict with society, persons incapable of loyalty, egotistical, insensitive, irresponsible, impulsive, incapable of feeling guilt or learning from an experience, demonstrating a low level of tolerance and a tendency to blame others. In criminal cases, this type of personality appears very frequently, and evidence indicates that the person affected by this social pathology is not able to establish a limit of respect in relation to other people, treating them as objects who can be manipulated as in a game of chess. This is the case, for example, of the *miche* (Brazilian term for a male prostitute), who attempts to take the life of his man, when feeling betrayed.

It would be useful to illustrate here with a concrete case.

Psychiatric studies now being developed by the English School, give the name *Sociopathy* to a personality disturbance affected by antisocial behavior, with the person having this pathology being called a *sociopath.* Guilherme de Pádua and his wife, Paula Thomaz, accused of the death of the brilliant actress Daniel Perez, a widely publicized fact that occurred in 1992 in Rio de Janeiro, would thus have what the English call *sociopathy,* exactly because they tried to destroy what they imagined was the reason for the insecurity and suffering in their social life. Daniela Perez represented everything that Guilherme de Pádua wanted to be, and, on the other hand, the strong ties of dependency between Guilherme de Pádua and his wife Paula Thomaz certainly heightened the pathological profile of both as accomplices in the brutal murder;

i. *passive-aggressive personality*—conduct marked by passivity and aggressiveness, which is frequently manifested passively through the habit of obstructionism, whims, laziness, ineffectiveness and obstinacy;

j. *inadequate personality*—conduct marked by social and family instability and difficulty in acting with good judgment, and may reveal a lack of willpower in actions and give ineffective responses to requests.

Sexual Deviancy

This involves psychosexual dysfunctions resulting from conflicts that lead to:

a. sexual interests for a person of the same sex;
b. practices of sexual acts not habitually associated with coitus;
c. coitus performed under strange circumstances.

Forms of sexual deviancy may include:

a. *narcissism*—satisfaction of the sexual instinct through contemplation of one's own body;
b. *homosexuality*—sexual attraction for a person of the same sex, with male homosexuality being called *uranism,* while female homosexuality is called *lesbism, lesbianism, tribadism* or *sapphism;*

c. *transvestism*—sexual perversion that leads the person to assume attitudes and clothing of the opposite sex;

d. *exhibitionism*—public exposure of the intimate parts of the body;

e. *fetichism*—sexual excitation motivated by material objects;

f. *pedophilia*—sexual attraction for a child;

g. *voyeurism, mixoscopy or espionism*—obtaining sexual satisfaction merely by contemplating sexual acts of others;

h. *sadism*—seeking orgasm through imposing physical or moral suffering on the partner;

i. *masochism*—satisfaction of the sex instinct through submitting to physical or moral suffering;

j. *satyrism* or *priapism*—morbid excitation of male sexuality, without the man feeling sexually satisfied;

k. *nymphomania* or *uteromania*—perversion which consists of exaggeration of female sexuality, which is why some say the woman has uterine furor;

l. *masturbation*—causing orgasm by means of auto-eroticism or solitary vice;

m. *auto-eroticism, erotomania* or *masturbation*—called psychic coitus, which leads to satisfaction of the sexual instinct only by mental evocation of erotic things;

n. *anaphrodisia*—diminution of the male sexual instinct, which may lead to impotency;

o. *frigidity*—diminution of the woman's sexual instinct;

p. *necrophilia* or *vampirism*—search for sexual satisfaction with cadavers;

q. *zoophylia* or *bestiality*—obtaining orgasm through sexual practices with animals;

r. *symptomatic state tending towards sexual deviancy*—has to due with occurrence of another possible type of sexual deviancy, brought about by symptomatology with a probability of arising in a person's daily life.

An example of "symptomatic state tending towards sexual deviancy" capable of causing personality disturbance is the typical profile of a man who, beginning at age forty, may become victim of the *age of the wolf* syndrome, also called *male menopause* or *andropause*. In this phase, the individual, as he questions his own model of sexual life and physical appearance, may develop the process of lack of self-criticism and exacerbation of the libido with intense frustrations and erotic fantasies. The fear of old age and the myth of impotence during the *age of the wolf* explain many shocking attitudes, such as searching for a much younger girlfriend, which brings a feeling of being rejuvenated, especially for those who cannot bear the idea of aging and begin a desperate search for their lost youth.

Alcoholism

This refers to patients whose alcohol consumption harms their physical health, as well as their personal and social activities, as a result of the morbid state resulting from abuse of alcoholic beverages.

Forms of alcoholism:

a. *episodic excessive alcohol ingestion*—In this situation alcoholism is present and the person becomes intoxicated several times during the year.

b. *habitual excessive alcohol ingestion*—Here the alcoholic becomes intoxicated with a resulting alteration in language, coordination or conduct. Generally, the person drinks more than once per week and many times during the year. The effects of alcohol are easily noticed, even if the person is not noticeably drunk.

c. *alcoholic addiction*—In this state the patient has a dependence on alcohol, to the point of suffering symptoms of withdrawal if there is a sudden suspension or reduction of dosage.

Drunkenness, the result of excessive ingestion of alcohol, presents three phases: euphoric, excitant and depressive.

Euphoric inebriation is the phase in which the subject feels intense happiness, becomes talkative and has a reduction in the capacity for self-criticism. This euphoric phase makes a person resemble a monkey.

Excited inebriation is the phase of mental confusion, marked by the appearance of disturbances in sensitivity, loss of motor coordination, constant irritation and difficulty in articulating words due to perturbation of nervous center. Excitation due due to intoxication by drink means that, in this phase, the individual resembles a lion.

Depressive inebriation is known as the sleep phase, in which there are neuropsychic disorders. During this period, the hallucinating drunk tends to sleep, and may fall into a state of coma. Since the person is completely prostrate in this phase, the similarity is to a pig, which falls and rolls in the mud.

Drug Dependency

This involves the patient who has a dependence on a medicine or psychotropic substance that acts on the psyche, as a sedative or a stimulant, altering the personality to a greater or lesser degree, depending on the hallucinogenic action that harms the body. As is known, psychotropic substances are divided into three groups. The classification below gives an idea of how they act:

I—the *psychocataleptics*—they act as depressants. They may be:
  a. hypnotic, such as barbituates;
  b. tranquilizers, such as the myorelaxants, the antihistamines, the acetilcolinics, the antihallucinatories,
  c. neuroleptics, such as chloropromazine;

II—the *psychoanalectics*—these are stimulants. They facilitate the action of chemical substances that regulate transmission of nervous impulses and enzymes. They can be:
  a. anti-hypnotics—such as amphetamine, Pervitim;
  b. antidepressants, such as Trofanil;

III—the *psychodyslethics*—these are depersonalizing.
  Other components distinguish the three groups of psychotropic drugs:
  a. among the psychocataleptics are the opiates: heroin, morphine and codein;
  b. among the psychoanalectics are cocaine and the anorexigenic drugs (appetite reducers);
  c. among the psychodyslethics are marijuana, hashish, lysergic acid and mescaline.

The patient may present dependency on opium, morphine, cocaine, barbituates, hypnotics, sedatives, tranquilizers, *cannabis sativa* and other psychostimulants, such as the amphetamines and certain hallucinogens.

One should note the peculiarity of identifying victims who live within criminality, generally in certain areas of the community, such as environments with levels of drug-dependency.

H.H. Brownstein, H.R. Baxi and P.J. Goldstein, dealing with the relation between drug addicts and drug dealers with the crime of homicide, affirm that the drug addicts' habits, which expose them to regularly being in "not very recommendable" environments, predispose them towards victimization. In that vein, these scholars demonstrate that even homicides that are not necessarily correlated with drugs, many times involve relations connected to them, not only established by the authors of homicides, but by their victims. To Brownstein, Baxi and Goldstein, there are very few innocent victims in those kinds of crimes.[1]

Note

1. These observations were presented by Professor Ana Paula Zomer, in an excellent presentation given at the First Interamerican Congress on Trial by Jury, held in São Paulo, during the period of March 15 to 17, 2000.

Chapter 5

The Victimogenous Core of the Victim's Personality

It is known that environmental differences impose on the personality a predominant layer of factors that influence in forming the human character. However, there is no denying that the origin for the condition of dangerousness, in both the criminal and the victim, has its axis in biopsychic characteristics that predispose and unleash antisocial actions, so that the crime is a mode of expressing the infractor's temperament or character.

This being the case, the ingredients of biological inheritance that make up the temperament and are expressed because of tendency, join with each other in relations that the personality has with the complex process of human existence in society, revealing the mode of being of the individual, his or her profile or psychological individuality, the "self" as an expression of will, sentiment, intelligence level, morality and attitudes towards life. Jose Ingenieros sums it up very well "the personality is the result of variations of inheritance faced with education by the character and manifests itself through conduct." (Ingenieros, 1919, p. 97). From this we may conclude that there are persons who are constitutionally unadaptable, even under favorable environmental situation, just as there are socioenvironmental circumstances that do not favor or impede the personality from distancing itself from the rules of coexistence dictated by social norms.

In a delinquent personality the identification of a given level of dangerousness is based on the **criminogeous core.** Following this same logic, in a victim's personality, identification of a certain level of dangerousness has its roots in the **victimogenous core** of the victimization process. In both poles of conduct, supporting levels of unconscious desires may appear, of lack of values or a certain dose of personal problems that come into conflict with family life and become adverse in the surrounding social environment.

Understanding the Victimogenous Core

The late lamented professor Heber Soares Vargas (1989, pp. 6-10) who honored the chair in Legal Medicine at the University of Londrina (Parana), without doubt one of the greatest expressions of the advances of Victimology in Brazil, was a pioneer in identifying the endo-psychic zoning of the victimogenous, illustrating it with the following graphic representation:

VICTIMOGENOUS CORE

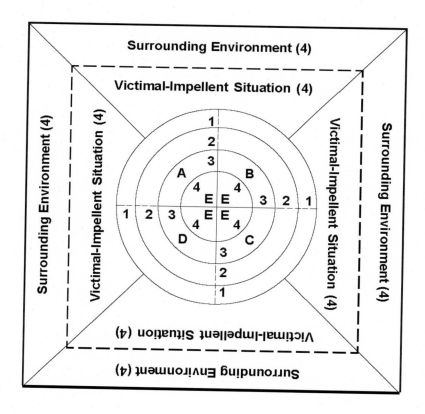

Here is professor Heber Soares Vargas' explanation of the victimogenous core:

> The diagram shows in an allegorical manner the victimogenous personality, which is a concept and measure derived from five components—Anxiety (A), Aggressiveness (B), Guilt Feelings (C), Masochism (D), Fragile Ego (E)—and the personal relations with the surrounding environment, in objective and subjective dependence on the victimal-impellent situation.
>
> Fields 1, 2, 3 and 4 represent the necessary agreements and accommodations between the bio-psychical demands of the body and the social demands of the environment. The victimogenous personality is an ingenious arrangement of those components engaged only in maintaining the defense mechanisms. All motivation and incentive coming from the surrounding environment occur directly upon the victimal-impellent causation, which acts on the personality by gradually energizing the existent fields, which indicate the sum of biosychosocial needs, interacting in an integrated manner on the specific components of the victimogenous personality that will reflect, in form, the individual's endopsychic conditions.
>
> Through the model proposed in this diagram, it may be seen that the components of the victimogenous personality are situated at certain levels within non-delimitated fields, because that combination, in combination with a fragile ego, corresponds to a need for psychofunctional adequacy.
>
> The low dominance of Anxiety (A) and of the Fragile Ego (E) could alternatively be due to a certain incompatibility between high emotive sensitivity and the consequences of a dominant behavior of affective insecurity. In the same way, the high dominance of the Guilt Feeling (C), Masochism (D) and Aggressiveness (B), united by the Fragile Ego (E) can incapacitate the individual in controlling victimizing impulses and emotions, and especially in finding a means of realistically and satisfactorily expressing them.
>
> No matter what specific interpretation one may adopt for explaining those components, the important thing is that one may observe a type of unitary influence of the personality that affects a whole structure of responses. What is perhaps most important is that those four components probably have their functional unity in the frailty of the ego, and absolute dependency and action, when they begin in field 1 to group

themselves, until field 4, where the frailty of the ego unites them into a single core, in other words, the victimogenous core.

Professor Heber Soares Vargas concludes:

The severe feeling of guilt and resulting masochism generally occupy the place of other causal factors in the favoring and in situations of precipitation, or even passive or active participation in the crime by the victim. In fact, the victim, by collaborating with commitment of a crime, be it in exposition to criminogenous circumstances, or even in those circumstances developed by his or her own action, wants to obtain psychic relief, even if it should come through a feeling of self-destruction and self-punishment. (Vargas, 1987, pp. 6-10)

With the victim, as also happens with the criminal, dangerousness varies in relation to the intensity of the action, direction of the purpose and other subjective and objective circumstances related to occurrence of the fact.

There are victims for whom practice of a crime represents a precise, determined activity. For others, practice of anti-social attitudes results from some non-adaptation. In both cases, victimal dangerousness, tied to conscious or unconscious motives, can break out due to stimuli coming from **pre-victimizing** or **victim-impellent** factors, bringing about unleashing of a dolose or culpose criminal act, depending on what actually occurs. Consequently, the state of victimal dangerousness happens every time that the moment of **victimogenous maturation** emerges, as happens in the same way with the criminal dangerousness of the delinquent, which is exhibited through **criminogenous maturation** that reveals an at-risk disposition, as happens with an underwater monster submerged in its watery lair, lurking in wait for its victims.

The forms of dangerousness for the victim are distinguished in groups of victimogenous situations identified as follows:

a. situations where the occasion makes possible acts of negligence, imprudence or ineptitude;
b. situations engendered by deliberate provocation of damage;
c. situations of exposure to real or imminent danger;
d. situations of aggressive psychopathic states and depressive states with desire for self-destruction or self-punishment;

e. situations of fixed ideas followed by repetitive attitudes that make obsessive or compulsive disturbances uncontrollable.

The manifestation of a dangerous state provides the victim with the opportunity to be characterized as principal active subject, co-participant or stimulator of the wrongdoing.

The victim's fearfulness is stereotyped with the list of symptoms coming from the victimogenous core of the personality, which acts as the driving force for creating results of damage or imminent peril. This process is begun when the person receives a stimulus from the surrounding environment or from his or her own inner world.

From the **victimogenous core,** as well as from the **criminogenous core**, then, come the impulses that will be externally presented, with levels of excitation or depression, aggressiveness, muteness, loneliness, emotional imbalance, lack of interest in things, rejection of persons, lack of interest in studies, resistance to working, lack of interest in the future or even in one's own life.

Observation of the human reality based on the victimogenous core, that is, on the threshold of the self's frailty in interaction with biopsychological or social factors, allows one to distinguish between the states of **victimal pre-dangerousness, pre-victimal dangerousness** and **victimal dangerousness.** Those states are easily detectible, for example, in analyzing conduct involved with drug dependence, which, at times, present both the existence of the **potential victim** (potentiality or availability to be a victim) as well as characterization of the victim-delinquent, who, in one form or the other, performs the role of infractor alone or involved with his or her aggressor's behavior.[1]

The diagnosis of victimal dangerousness may be established with the identification of two basic presuppositions:

a. victim's degree of individual integration;
b. victimogenous capacity.

The degree of individual integration consists of understanding the diversity of biopsychological reactions when faced with conscious or unconscious conflicts, born from the individual-individual and individual-environment reaction.

Victimogenous capacity is understood to be the result of action, on a greater or lesser scale, of the personality's victimogenous core, together with the predispositoions and motivations that lead the individual towards victimogenous behavior. Thus, the victimogenous capacity encompasses elements of the victimogenous core (anxiety, guilt feeling, masochism, hetero and self-aggression), which interrelate and become sources of anti-social conduct, mainly if there is contagion from external factors, which help to make hidden images of the personality become visible.

Since humans are social creatures, assessment of their process of integration into society should not leave out an examination of psycho-homeostasis (the self-regulatory property that allows the individual to maintain a highly personalized balance), considering the discipline dictated by the structure of the ego. The better the person's integration into the environment (family and social), the better structured will be the mechanisms regulating the human ego. Consequently, having a strong ego means having good psycho-homeostasis integration; having a fragile ego means having poor psycho-homeostasis integration. If the ego is fragile, the victimogenous core increases in proportion to the capacity for self-victimization, generating the elements that structure the flow of victimal dangerousness.

Origin of the Guilt Feeling

The philosopher Friedrich Nietzsche, and after him, Sigmund Freud vigorously studied the origin of the guilt feeling as found in Psychological Science (Koffka, 1933, pp. 670-676). Its origin is founded on the fact that, for both, the passage from nature to culture and the establishment of the human kingdom come about through the violent repression of impulses that had become incompatible with civilizing ideals. This also means, in other dimensions, the presupposition that an unconscious motivation is present in the actions of individuals and peoples. In that perspective, the state of society is not the result of a contract or a peaceful conquest for the higher faculties, nor does it mean reason dominating the *animal* part inside each one of us. To the contrary, it is a struggle, conflict, violence, whose result is a growing process of accommodation, adaptation and domestication. Now it is inside this process that the need for producing guilt is lodged.

In his work "Genealogy of Morals" (1887), Nietzsche describes the violence of this process, which consists of turning a person into "an animal capable of making promises," through creating of a *memory*, that will remind us at every moment of the *debts* that we contract. *Debt* here is a key word, which in German, not by chance, is written as *Schuld,* a word that also means *guilt*. It is the creditor-debtor relation that, in this sense, brings civilization into being. No mechanical solidarity, no gregarious instinct leads us to constitute a society, but the implacable struggle between two sentiments, that of responsibility and that of blame, where one is either creditor or debtor. Out of this struggle morality is established. Good and bad, saints and sinners, are characteristics, interventions, forms of life, that result from the ideals of morality (Alexander, 1932, p. 79).

Both Freud and Nietzsche have shown that the feeling of guilt comes from the anguish of facing authority (especially paternal) and anguish before the *Superego*. The former comes about by constraining the subject to renounce drives and desires, the latter by making it impossible to hide from the *Superego* the persistence of those desires, which leads us to constant self-punishment. The *Superego,* in this way, prolongs, intensifies, externalizes and makes external severity partly unconscious. From thence arises the feeling of guilt, of having committed a fault, and it is in that other struggle, between desire and prohibition, that the moral conscience is formed (Freud, 1968, pp. 412-417).

This being the case, what both authors highlight is this inalienable mark of guilt, this bitter taste of pain and suffering that runs through our culture. It is because we well guilty that we affirm so peremptorily that "only suffering can teach us." With that, we frequently drag other people into a pain that is ours and create a hellish circle of repeated guilt, where all are guilty, where everyone owes someone something. And where all sicken: of resentment, says Nietzsche; of neurosis, says Freud (Freud, 1968, pp. 421).

As is known, Freud distinguished the three structures of the soul: the *Id* (das *Es*), the *Ego* (das *Ich*) and the *Superego* (das *Uberich*). The *Id* is the domain of the unconscious. It is made up of atavistic tendencies, primary instincts and childhood repressions. It has nothing to do with logic or ethics and operates in an irrational manner, motivated solely by pleasure. When the *Id* comes into conflict with the demands of the outside world, the *Ego* appears, arising from perception and capable of reasoning. Through it are expressed the tendencies of the *Id*, which it takes over and transforms into actions. It exercises *censorship* of impulses and represses those that should not come to the surface. If conflict arises between the freed and repressed impulses, neurosis appears. Psychological processes differ from individual to individual, with each one giving rose to a coherent and organic disposition, which is the personality. The education given by parents and teachers, Freud points out, introduces into children certain characteristics that will generate the *Super-ego*, whose role is to keep watch over any attempt of the *Ego*, when the latter should allow the manifestation of anything arising from repressed childhood sexuality (Freud, 1968, pp. 417-423).

PROPULSION TOWARDS CRIME OR VICTIMIZATION

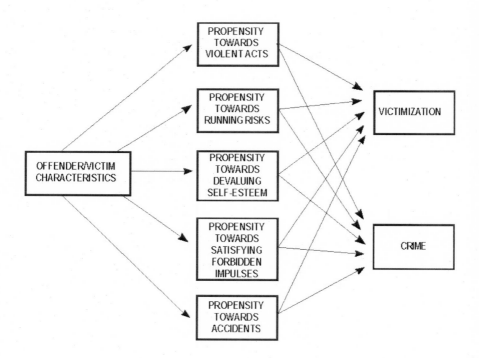

Notes

1. The social unease that arises from the predisposition towards being a victim can lead to the "judgement of *victimal dangerousness*, since the victim becomes part of the group of subjects who can be the target of a security measure, because he is the creator of disturbances to the public order, when, to some degree, he instigates wrongdoing or contraventions, and should thus be protected from the damaging event unleashed by his special nature." (Castro, 1969, p. 66)

Chapter 6

The Victimological Examination

Precipitation towards crime may provide, in some cases, an overall assessment of the victim's highly personalized conditions, as occurs with the criminological examination with its purpose of obtaining specific data on the personality and state of dangerousness of the delinquent.

Purpose of the Victimological Examination

To define the victimological examination, it has the purpose of researching factors related to personal, family and social background, in terms of physical-psychic, psychological, social and environmental aspects, to obtain data indicative of the temperament and character that make up the victim's personality and may reveal the existence of a certain degree of dangerousness.

Identifying conduct that bears a tendency towards precipitating crime requires an overall assessment of the victim's highly personalized aspects, so as to uncover authentic practices and real casuistic guidelines that will enable better orientation for a judicial decision.

With the concrete function of identifying any hypothesis as to the type of victim, no work can do without providing an important role for the methods of victimological investigation. Thus, with our precise objectives in mind, the total picture of a personality possessing a special inclination towards antisocial acts, will never be definitively established without an authorized performance of the scientific examination.

Investigating anomalies, whatever they may be, through analysis of endogenous and exogenous factors, is a primary function of modern Victimology and solidifies the ever growing alliance between Criminal

Law and the other sciences concerned with resolving enigmas directly or indirectly linked to human life (Versele, 1962, pp. 595-604).

Since the Judge is not required to be an expert in Criminology or Victimology, he or she needs enlightened advice provided by doctors, psychologists, sociologists, anthropologists, psychoanalysts, social workers and other specialists, who, through methods of observation, will provide a diagnosis of the victim's personality to identify his or her level of involvement with the criminal, thus enabling a clear judgment of the dangerousness that she or he carries.

Convenience of the Victimological Examination

To minimize the inconveniences of the victimological examination there should be a preponderant formula whereby the experts can only examine the victim if he or she consents and by means of authorization from the Judge, who must take every precaution to avoid exaggerated invasion of the victim's intimacy and not allow the experts to nose around in the most hidden corners of a human being.

We must make it clear that we do not defend a victimological examination directed towards any type of crime or for every type of victim. The examination will only be opportune in highly special circumstances when it is absolutely indispensable to clarify certain situations, above all those with enormous social repercussions, so long as one has the agreement of the victim to submit to a carefully measured assessment that is capable of forming an overall judgment of his or her personality.

Regarding the appropriateness of the exam, we must caution that one must pay attention to the real possibilities in each country. In Brazil, for example, if would be absolutely impossible to make a victimological examination obligatory, given that not all States have material and human conditions for developing scientific activities in personality investigation, especially in the more distant hinterland regions. Since it is not prudent to place in the law a precept obligating the Judge, it is best to leave to the Judges discretion and best conscience, the power of determining or not an examination, as long as there is consent from the victim.

Legitimacy of the Victimological Examination

As to legitimacy, we hold that the victimological examination should be allowed, as long as it is surrounded by confidentiality and precautions for safeguarding human dignity.

It would be inconsistent to defend that the investigation not look into intimate human aspects, but that does not mean allowing violation of privacy, since that can bring damages and distress to the person's psychic structure, as well as to the standing her or she enjoys in the community. It is even absurd to speak of a typology or classification of victims, without prudently and competently preparing for each type a series of examinations that will identify their characteristics and recommend adequate treatment, with discretion, to the benefit of the person. Publicity should be banned so as to not expose the examinee to embarrassing situations and not to encourage social stigmas.

Usefulness of the Victimological Examination

Besides favoring the victim, allowing him or her a new route of conduct, an additional use of the examination is that it brings positive results for a healthy crime prevention policy adopted for the benefit of society.

Assessment of actions in the surroundings and reactions in the environment must deal with everything that characterizes and qualifies behavior: family, customs, habits, profession, learning, degree of culture, friendship connections, economic situation, etc. This means one must not forgo evaluating an individual born in privileged circumstances, with a solid projection in intellectual and social life, with the same technical standards used to analyze a person born in a humble home or a slum, who has never had chances for social and economic projection.

This aspect is fundamental for forming a judgment of the victim, since, given that human behavior is the product of roots in biological nature and social nature, the appropriate prophylactic and re-educational methods must be based on an integral knowledge of the personality, through its static and dynamic, somatic and psychological aspects, so as to provide conditions for efficient combat of the baneful origins of existing situations.

Scope of the Victimological Examination

The exam must provide a multidimensional observation that will allow one to achieve an image of the victim.

In analyzing personal background one must examine the biological factor, the animic factor, the hylemorphic factor and the moral factor. The report of the physical and psychic investigation is purely descriptive. Generally, the technicians adopt some biotypology to speak of the biotypology to which the person being examined belongs.

The morphocharacteriological focus proposes to find, by means of certain somatic aspects, eventual psychic correspondences. That concern has led some students in the field to prepare classifications of certain types with the use of anthropometric data, which has led to a major expansion not only of the conclusions presented by the development of Criminal Biotypology, but also of Criminal Biology and Criminal Endocrinology (Berardinelli, 1936, pp. 448-456.).

For both the criminologist and the victimologist, knowledge of the contributions offered by Biotypology is indispensable, which can now offer precise information of the biological peculiarities of individual constitution. Performance of crimino-biological research is extremely important for classifying criminals or victims with a view to applying effective measures for social defense.

Some time ago the German techniques employed a more fundamentally biological orientation in establishing diagnoses and prognoses for the personality. For their part, specialists in the United States have always sought to highlight more the sociological factor. In recent years, criminological and victimological studies in general have demonstrated that each of the two factors has a specific importance, depending on the objectives sought, in isolated analyses of the cases presented (Barkan, 1997, 100-105).

There is no concrete separation allowing one to affirm that there is a purely social or purely individual part of the personality. The psychologist, the sociologist, the anthropologist and the doctor all have their justifications for their viewpoints, but all must freely recognize the numerous points of intersection and the mutual interdependence of the two structures.

In examining the family background it is importance to see which genetic and which environmental factors have influenced the family.

In investigating the somatic constitution, one must especially take into account the perversions, deformities, and, also, the ethnic group of the examinee, not specifically from an ethnic aspect, but because of the habits, customs, traditions and mentality of each people.

Psychologist Gordon Allport, when analyzing the cultural environment, in terms of the status and reference in which the personality develops, notes that "in a certain manner, it is determined by conventions, customs and social codes, which means that a large part of man's nature tends to be a reflection of those norms." Knowledge of the way people participate in groups is the best element for predicting their future conduct. "However, it is never enough to have a simple report on socio-cultural participation, for no individual isolatedly reflects his participation in the community, his religious posture or his social class. The personality, as we have insisted, is something more than the subjective side of culture, a truth that some social scientists tend to forget" (Allport, 1974, pp. 491-493).

Knowledge of the relation between somatic and psychic makeup requires an investigation into the reciprocal influence of temperament and character, since a complete examination requires investigation of the hylemorphic aspects, that is, the factors linked to body and spirit. The temperament together with intelligence and physical aspects are the parts of the personality that most depend on the hereditary factor, which allows us to understand that the personality is, to a large degree, conditioned by the temperament, although minute details of this affirmation still depend on more research in the genetic, biochemical, neurological, endocrine and physical anthropology sectors.

As to character, when we speak of it we mean the moral standards of a person, which is why the concept of character as *valued personality* is very well known. The character is the mark imprinted on the personality, that is modified according to evolution. Plato used to say that "the good man, a lover of order and harmony, who is lapidated throughout his lifetime, is a jeweler, whose masterpiece is himself." Thus, every evil inclination that we bring with us at birth, must be corrected with the improvement of character, with the educational work of parents and teachers in specialized formation and the school of life being indispensable in this regard.

In constructing an ethnic judgment, we must view the limits and modifiers of imputability, as is taught with notable wisdom, by Italian professor Bernardino Alimena (1984, pp. 347-356). Here there must be a focus on all points linked to diseases of the spirit, to sleepwalking, to hypnotism, to suggestion, to deaf-muteness, to drunkenness, to age, to sex, to ignorance, to error, to emotion, to passion, to fear, to rage and to pain.

A constitutional and physiological assessment, as Norman Munn has well observed, requires exams of glandular and autonomous functions, psycho-galvanic skin reflexes, lung volume, heart capacity, arterial tension, blood group, visual and auditory acuity, muscular force, brain waves and other fundamental functions of the physical structure (Munn, 1951, p. 347).

Science currently offers us the possibility of obtaining precise measures of physiological functions with electronic polygraphs. Today, with advances in scientific experiments, it is possible to analyze the influence of genetic factors, studying heredity through graphs of family records used by eugenics associations. The secrets of the genetic code involving microscopic particles known as chromosomes, have a maximum correlation with knowledge of anomalies, implications and difficulties exposed by human hereditary characteristics, particularly in the field of criminal problems, given that there is a growing body of scientific research pointing to genetic influence as a determining or co-participant factor in conduct and behavioral deviancies that display aggressive and even violent impulses (Vernet, 1968, pp. 207-217).

In biological investigations, psychiatric-type exams using electroencephalography have been highly significant for applying justice, given that the Criminal Court Judge needs to know the psychic conditioning factors of the delinquent's behavior. The electroencephalogram technique consists of registring the differences in electric potential that may occur between the brain's nerve cells, is also quite advanced, and thanks to it, it seems to be established that abnormal brain waves are frequently found in forms of psychopathic personalities (Di Tullio, 1954, p. 134).

It should be pointed out that scientists, concerned with the influences of constitutional and morphological factors on temperament and character, have, since the end of the XIX century, demonstrated conclusions of exams done on the state of human delinquency, but these still do not allow one, despite scientific progress in criminological and victimological concepts, to unquestionably conceive of the existence of a typical morphology for victims or criminals.

Criminal Endocrinology, for example, has been trying to prepare a typology that relates the endocrine forms of an individual with his or her psychic form. The authors point out to *Dalla Medicina Alla Sociologia,* a work published in Palermo, Italy in 1922 by Nicola Pende, as initial work for the endocrinology movement in terms of the study of criminality. Endocrinologists have used endocrine infirmities caused by excess or scarcity to classify temperaments in terms of hyper or hypo-functioning of the pituitary, pineal, thyroid, parathyroid, thymus and suprarenal glands, gonads and insular tissue in the pancreas.

Bio-psycho-criminogenetic observation is as important as the dynamics of human behavior and respective social engagement. So as to judge appropriately, the Criminal Court judge needs to know about the family, professional and friendship relations of the accused, in order to build an idea of his or her background in terms of sociability and anti-sociability (Sykes, 1961, pp. 51-53).

Besides the collaboration of teachers, social workers, sociologists and anthropologists, participation by a psychologist is extremely important, since, in order to analyze the various elements that make up the personality, it is not enough for the psychologist to point out an isolated characteristic of the volitional aspect. There must be a precise definition of how all those factors are processed and interconnected.

Making a comparison with chemistry, we could reach the conclusion that the personality is a given compound, as is sulfuric acid. This is a compound of hydrogen, sulfur and oxygen, and it would thus be erroneous to affirm that one could prove that only one of those elements is sulfuric acid itself (H_2SO_4). When we combine two parts of hydrogen, one part of sulfur and four parts of oxygen, we obtain a new body, which is not any of its components. To analyze this new body, we need to verify all of its components, which result in a synthesis, in the same way as happens with the personality.

In the following graph, we present a summary of the convergent requirements of the victimological examination.

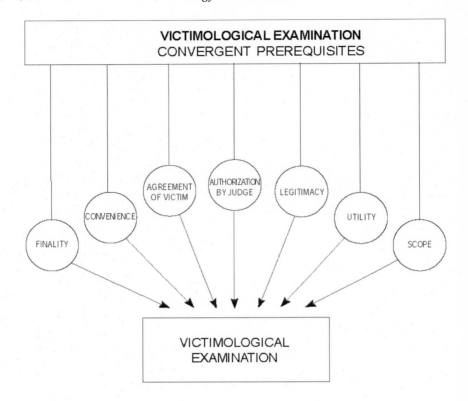

Chapter 7

The *Iter Victimae*—The Path to Victimization

Iter Victimae is the term used to designate the internal and external path followed by an individual in becoming a victim.

In order to have a clear understanding of the *Iter Victima* and its comparison with the *Iter Criminis*, there needs to be a prior analysis of the parallel path traveled on the other side by the characters in the crime, so as to clearly establish the peculiarities having to do with the *Iter Criminis* and those that relate to the *Iter Victimae*, clearly a major concern in examining the victim's position when applying modern criminal proceedings (Schneider, 1988, pp. 74-79).

Phases of the *Iter Criminis*

Iter Criminis is the trajectory followed by the author in the dynamics of developing a misdeed.

The basic phases of *Iter Criminis* are: a) cogitation; b) preparatory acts; c) beginning of execution; d) execution; e) consummation or attempt.

Cogitation (*Cogitatio*)

This is the first moment in the *Iter Criminis*, during which the agent plots out what to do (ideation) to make the decision of practicing the misdeed or not. It is not a punishable fact, because it is not projected to the outside world.

In Ancient Rome a maxim of Ulpianus became famous and is today enshrined as a universal principle of judicial logic: *nemo poenam patitur* (thoughts do not pay taxes or obey law).

Cogitation, therefore, its the initial phase of the crime trajectory, and is judicially irrelevant.

In this stage it is important to distinguish the finality of the operation (*fins operis*) and the purpose for which the agent cogitates the crime (*finis operantis*). That happens with all human actions. A sculptor carves a statue to embellish a tomb and, with that, achieve glory. The first consequence, decorating the tomb, is the finality of the operation; the second, achieving glory, is the artist's purpose. In the same way, in the world of crime, one may distinguish the finality of the criminal act and what the agent had as a target. Thus, for example, in the crime of active corruption (article 333 of the Brazilian Penal Code—CP), the finality of the action is getting the employee to practice, omit or delay an official act, while the finality of the agent is to obtain profit from this.

Preparatory Acts (*Conatus Remotus*)

After cogitation the crime, the agent enters into preparatory acts, wherein to obtain the means, instruments, predisposition of modes and the choice of the occasion for carrying out the crime. Example: drawing a dagger, aiming a firearm. These are normally judicially irrelevant, because at those moments there is still no effective beginning in effectively carrying out the crime. But exceptions are provided within penal dogmatics, where legislators have decided to transform certain preparatory acts into autonomous crimes. Examples: a) simulating the authority to perform weddings (article 238, CP); b) manufacturing explosives or toxic gas (article 253, CP); c) incitement by means of words, gestures, writings or other expression, that implies instigation towards practicing a crime (article 286, CP); d) association of more than three persons in a gang or band (article 288, CP); e) fabrication of an apparatus or any object for counterfeiting money (article 291, CP). In the five cases above, the preparatory acts destined for practicing other misdeeds, initiate typical conduct.

Beginning of Execution (*Conatus Proximus*)

After preparing, the agent moves towards beginning execution, at which moments he or she begins to carry out the activity that constitutes a definitive crime under law. Here lies the beginning of punishable illicitness. Examples: placing poison in food; firing a weapon.

Execution (*Executio*)

This is the development of action in a necessary and sufficient manner to achieve the result. Examples: the victim takes the poison; is hit by the bullet fired.

Consummation (Goal Achieved or *Consummatio*)

This represents achievement of the result, in other words, of the event that corresponds to complete realization of the typical conduct (article 14, I, CP). With consummation, the agent carries out, in all terms, the legal type of wrongdoing figure; that is, a legal good protected under criminal law has received effective damage or even a threat, which is expressed through a type of crime. Examples: death of the victim (article 121, CP); danger of venereal contagion (article 130, CP).

Attempt (Unsuccessful Crime or *Conatus Proximus*)

It is considered an attempted crime when, in carrying out the fact, the agent begins to act, intending to achieve the event, which does not come about due to circumstances that are against his or her will (article 14, II, CP). Example: the agent shoots but the victim is able to avoid the bullet by falling to the ground.

Phases of the *Iter Victimae*

As has already been described, *Iter Victimae* is the set of phases that operate chronologically in developing the victimization process.

Intuition (*Intuito*)

The first *Iter Victimae* is intuition, when the idea of being harmed, opposed, or killed by an offender is first planted in the victim's mind.

Preparatory Acts (*Conatus Remotus*)

After mentally projecting the expectation of being a victim, the individual enters the preparatory acts phase (*conatus remotus*), in which he or she carefully takes preliminary measures to defend her or himself or adjusts his or her behavior, so as to consensually or resignedly adjust behavior to the designs for damage or danger articulated by the offender.

Beginning of Execution (*Conatus Proximus*)

Later on comes the phase of beginning execution (*conatus proximus*), at which moment the victim begins putting a defense into operation, taking advantage of the chance to do so, or directing his or her behavior towards cooperating, supporting or facilitating the action or omission desired by the offender.

Execution (*Executio*)

Next comes the actual carrying out of the crime, distinguished by definitive resistance by the victim to avoid at all cost being impacted by the result intended by the aggressor, or by allowing him or herself to be victimized.

Consummation (*Consummatio*) or Attempt (Unsuccessful Crime or *Conatus Proximus*)

Finally, after *execution,* there is *consummation,* through achievement of the effect pursued by the author, with or without adhesion by the victim. If repulsion from the victim is encountered during *execution*, the result may be an *attempted crime*, when the practice of the fact demonstrates that the author did not achieve his or her purpose (*finis operantis*) because of some impediment against his or her will.

The graph on the following page summarizes the path to crime and the path to victimization.

Victim/Offender Crossing Schemes

Also as part of the focus related to the *Iter Victimae*, the Mexican professor Luís Rodriguez Manzanera has prepared a series of interesting diagrams to clearly illustrate the lines projected by the offender and by the victim, in the complex of convergent or divergent stages that these personages put into effect during the criminal enterprise (Manzanera, 1988, pp. 143-146).

THE PATH TO CRIME AND THE PATH TO VICTIMIZATION
ITER CRIMINIS

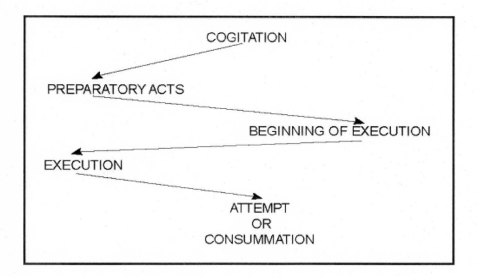

ITER VICTIMAE

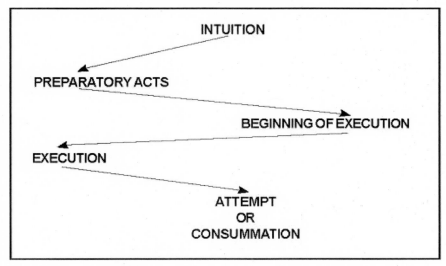

Professor Manzanera's schemes are ordered in harmony with the graphic representation of the seven diagrams shown in the following pages:

  a. *First scheme*: victim and offender follow different paths and itineraries;
  b. *Second scheme*: the offender performs the finished criminal act, obtaining the desired benefit from the crime;
  c. *Third scheme*: the *Iter Criminis* is completed with a last act for the offender;
  d. *Fourth scheme*: the victim follows the offender's path;
  e. *Fifth scheme*: the offender follows the victim's path;
  f. *Sixth scheme*: the person becomes a victim as a result of a culpose crime;
  g. *Seventh scheme*: the victim takes revenge on the offender.

Victim/Offender Crossing

First scheme: victim and offender cross paths, but each goes his or her own way, with different itineraries according to their personal interests and convenience. Example: active and passive corruption.

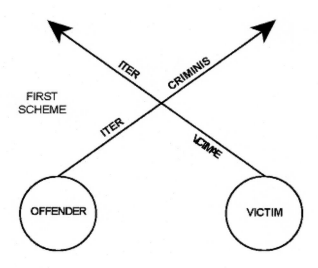

Second scheme: the *Iter Victimae* ends with complete realization of the crime in relation to the victim (finished criminal acts), in which opportunity the offender obtains the desired profit from the crime, closing the causal nexus linking the conduct to the event. Example: homicide, theft.

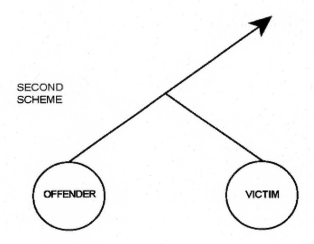

Third scheme: the *Iter Criminis* is completed with a final act for the offender. Example: death of the aggressor, when the offended party reacts in legitimate self defense

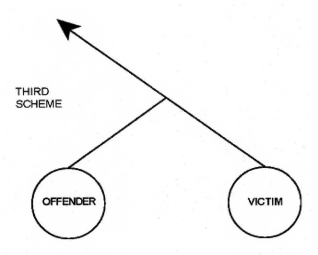

Fourth scheme: The victim follows the path of the offender. Example: a rape victim who latter becomes a prostitute with the help of the aggressor.

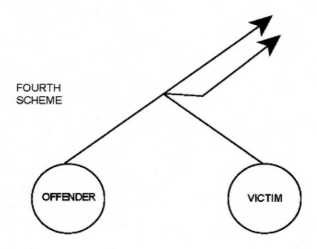

Fifth scheme: the offender follows the path of the victim. Example: the sexual violator who, to avoid conviction, marries the victim.

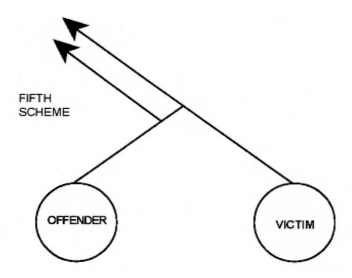

Sixth scheme: the person becomes a victim without having been deliberately chosen for that role, but due to negligence, imprudence or ineptitude (culpose crime) caused by lack of diligence on the part of the offender. Example: a traffic accident.

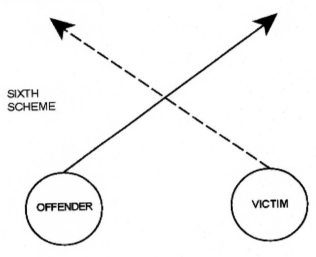

Seventh scheme: the victim crosses paths with the offender and initiates a path of revenge against him or her. Example: reaction to blackmail.

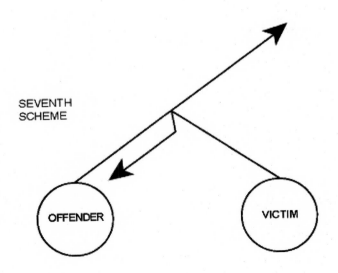

Chapter 8

Repeat Victimization

When we speak of repeat victimization, we are referring to the probability of a person being victimized by reiterated criminal acts, in other words, a victim subjected to repeated aggression.

Research on Repeat Victims

The first empirical research on repeat victimization occurred in 1978, in Cambridge, Massachusetts. Professor Michael Hindelang, coordinator of a group of researchers (Hindelang, Gottredson & Garofalo, 1978, pp. 16-21), found that the victims were not being appropriately catalogued in the context of population statistics. This consequently generated a mistake in disseminating the quantitative numbers of victimized people, especially because the fact that many had been affected several times in specific crime events at various times and places had not been considered.[1]

To establish the probability of repeat victimization, Ken Pease and Graham Farrell, in 1993, performed an analysis involving cases of victimizations occurring in England in 1982, 1988 and 1992. In 1982, 68% of the population was not victimized. On the other hand, 14% of the population was victimized more than once; these events accounted for 71% of the total number of crimes examined. Evaluations of data from 1988 and 1992 showed the same tendency (Pease & Farrell, 1993, p. 46). Belgian professor Jean Van Dijk has noted research carried out in several Western European countries from 1996 to 1999, presenting similar results. Those studies provide an interesting clue for specific prevention against continued thefts an robberies in at-risk neighborhoods, involving situations of persons who have been victimized more than once (Van Dijk, 1999, pp. 16-38).

In 1992, Professor Ralph Burquest commanded an investigation based on Police data on 33 primary and secondary schools in the city of Merseyside, England. It was found that of 296 events recorded, 263 involved repeat victimization, that is, 97.6% of the total.

Looking at the relation between racism and violence, Alice Sampson and Coretta Phillips in 1992 also released statistics of a survey of racial attacks in East London. During a six-month period they interviewed a number of poor families; of those, 67% had been victimized several times.

Comparing Ralph Burquest's research with the results of the Alice Sampson and Coretta Phillips research on racism, one may see that the two reached the same conclusion: the highest risk of repeat victimization occurs immediately after the first occurrence.

Research currently being carried out in the United Kingdom related to *repeat victims* has aided Judges in the task of better applying Criminal Law. They seek to operate with due care in at-risk regions, to keep a first victimization from being the prelude to a second, considering the circumstance that the victim of a crime has a strong susceptibility to being victimized again. British judges also take into consideration the circumstance that, after the first victimization, the probability of a second attempt y the aggressor is three times higher than the first (Sampson & Phillips, 1992, p. 36).

At the University of Pennsylvania in the United States, another interesting study has revealed that repeat victimization commonly tends to occur with crimes where there is a relation between the victim and the guilty party, as happens in the cases of conjugal aggression, domestic violence, or excesses in work relations. Four examples: the wife frequently tortured by her husband; the stepfather who routinely mistreats the child of his wife's previous marriage, incest, and a boss who successively humiliates an employee.

Typical Incidences of Repeat Victimization

In regard to all of the evidences cited here, it is important to note that repeat victimization is not necessarily limited to the same type of crime, be it against the person, against individual freedom or against patrimony. Professor Jean Van Dijk, poring over data from various victimology studies in Western Europe and the United States, verified that 42% of victimized or victimizable persons (subject to victimization) are attracted to a crime of a different nature, after consummation of a first nexus of causality between conduct by the author and the resulting event (Van Dijk, 2001, pp. 28-41).

In the sphere of International Law, the current scenario of terrorism fits the repeat victimization model, because it is a strong example of violent repetition (Winer, 2002, pp. 23-26).

In the chapter on *Hypotheses for Precipitation or Programming of the Crime by the Victim*, we situate specific types of victimogenous conduct, in which it is possible to note peculiarities that frequently characterize repeat victimization.

Here are some of those peculiarities:

a. victim due to affective necessity, characterized by the victomogenous character of certain sexual partners, who convert or reduce someone to the condition of victim/

b. victim of blackmail, who falls into the trap of an extortionist or blackmailer;

c. victim of fraudulent maneuvers who delivers his or her assets to a clever swindler;

d. victim of a crime against honor, through dissemination of facts and details regarding a person's individuality or privacy;

e. victim of drug consumption, destroyed by the drug dealer's coldness or impulsiveness;

f. victim of a medical crime, which places the patient in danger or brings about effective damages.

Origin of Repeat Victimization

Three hypotheses (Pease, 1998, pp. 90-92) have been formulated to explain the origin of repeat victimization;

First hypothesis: predisposition. The risk may result from a predisposition. As we explained earlier in focusing on the *Stereotype of Delinquent/Victim Interaction*, Professor Hans von Henting at Yale University was the person who structured the conception of *latent victim*, a person who has a predisposition or inclination to be victimized (Henting, 1948, pp. 408-413). It is not a question of saying someone is a *natural-*

born victim,[2] but a *victim due to tendency*, affected through a reduction in organic resistance, due to a combination of biological or mesological forces, which lead the person to slip up, due to his or her own frailty, going beyond the threshold of critical sense.

No person is born with a hereditary predestination to be a *natural-born victim*, but only with the probability of fitting in with the nature of a given victimogenous conduct (Baril, 1984, no. 2, pp. 13-18). The *natural-born victim* thesis is destroyed by paying due attention to the reasoning that it is behavior—much more than personal characteristics—that allows one to assess a victim's culpability, on a scale going from total innocence to full liability. A human being does not come into the world inexorably fated to be a victim or delinquent.

One can thus make a clear argument for a predisposition towards a *second victimization*. The psychic response due to having been the target of rejection or disdain after the first violence suffered, can lead the victim to a process of impotence, isolation and stress that stimulate a predisposition towards a *second victimization*. In this regard, certain victims of crime—kidnapping, armed robbery or severe sexual violation—exhibit psychopathologies such as post-traumatic shock, panic syndrome, agoraphobia and depressive anomaly, which, without due assistance and appropriate treatment for psychic restructuring, precipitate a second victimization, which, for its part, provides momentum for *repeat victimization* (Denkers, pp. 64-77).

Second Hypothesis. The delinquents return to the crime scene to recover lost or hidden objects, erase clues or proof of authorship, threaten or eliminate the victim, or because they think that location is the easiest or most convenient for repeating the desired crime.

Third Hypothesis. The delinquents, in their own language, pass on information to other delinquents, showing them the route for acting in certain zones that are propitious or advantageous for executing and consummating the crime.

The three hypotheses above suggest the design of a geographic chart, pointing out areas where one can detect the concentration of types of criminality, especially those involving multiple victimization. The knowledge of those crime rates favors preventive action through an appropriate anti-crime policy and an effective victimological policy (Fattah, 2001, vol. 1, pp. 63-81).

The anti-crime policy will be better oriented, in the sense of enabling the Police to fulfill their mission more efficiently, by observing above all, that repeat victims live with a more intense fear and feel more unprotected than persons victimized only once.

For its part, victimological policy needs to be more consistent. It has the possibility of being guided through public and private programs implemented by entities, associations and special victim assistance groups.[3] It may also be done through scientific analyses, working with a test that will adduce if it is the situation or the person that generates the possibility of multiple victimization. In other words, it needs to be clarified whether it is the first victimal occurrence that causes the risk of subsequent victimization, or it is the person who is more susceptible of becoming a victim again.

In summary, crime prevention and aid to the victims are indissoluble rights, given the need citizens have for public safety, as well defined practices of respect for human rights, which is why they are indispensable in democratic societies.

Notes

1. *Victimality* is in counterpoint to the expression *criminality*, which is the set of antisocial conduct and actions that indicate the volume of crimes within a given context.

2. In the item on *Stereotype of Delinquent/Victim Interaction*, we showed that Severin Versele, a Belgian professor and researcher, was the one who projected the conception of *natural-born victim*.

3. According to an orientation provided in Resolution number 4034, of November 29, 1985, of the UN General Assembly, which established the *Declaration of Fundamental Principles of Justice Related to Victims of Criminality and Victims of Abuse of Power*.

Chapter 9

Hypotheses for the Victim Precipitating or Programming the Crime

From August 28 to September 1, 1988, the VI International Symposium on Victimology was held in Jerusalem, in which I had the honor of participating, presenting the thesis of *victim precipitated crime*. In that critical presentation, I showed that it is not fair to continue to apply to all concrete cases a black and white portrait in which the criminal is always evil and inconsequential, while the victim is habitually pure and innocent, when, in effect, the roles may be inverted in unleashing impulses and in the flow of **criminal-impellent** or **victim-impellent** factors, which Benigno Di Tullio has described (Di Tullio, 1963, p. 96). **Criminal-impellent** factors have to do with impulses for a criminal attitude. **Victim-impellent** factors have to do with impulses towards a victimal situation, and from there one may note opportunities in which, under any pretext, the victim proposes to prepare or program the coordinates of his or her own victimization.

It is obvious and incontestable that we recognize the existence of so many innocent victims, many of who are submitted to the suffering of sacrifice and testing.

In reading the Book of Genesis, we see that, in those days, God put Abraham to the test. Calling him, he said, "Abraham!" And he answered "Here am I." And God said "Take your only son, Isaac, whom you love so much, go to the land of Moriah, and offer him there as a holocaust on a mountain that I shall show you."

When they reached the place shown to them by God, Abraham built an altar, placed the wood on top of it, tied up his son and placed him on top of the wood on the altar. Then, reaching out his hand, he took up his knife to sacrifice his son.

Then the angel of the Lord cried out from heaven, saying, "Abraham! Abraham!" He answered "Here am I." And God said "Do not lay a hand on your son and do him no harm! Now I know that you fear God, since you have not refused me your own son." Abraham lifted up his eyes, saw a ram caught by its horns in a thicket; he went and took it and offered it as a burnt offering in place of his son.

The angel of the Lord called to Abraham a second time from heaven and said to him, "I swear by myself—the Lord's own word—that since you have acted this way and not refused me your only son, I will bless you and make your descendents as numerous as the stars in the sky and the sands on the seashore."

With the progress of technical investigations, one concludes that the authors of crimes are really responsible, according to how their conduct is involved, when there is practice of an act, defined by law as a malicious or culpable crime. Everything depends on how the author's behavior is acted out. In my book *Comentários ao Código Penal (Comments on the Penal Code)* I have treated this issue in greater depth (Oliveira, 2005, pp. 265-269).

Malice is the desire to carry out a given type of conduct, encompassing that which the author intends to achieve as the objective of his or her action: the exact result projected for performing the typical conduct (direct malice) or the probable result that she or he assumed the risk of producing (eventual malice).

The Brazilian Penal Code places direct malice on the same line as eventual malice (article 18, I), but in essence direct malice reveals a greater determination and recklessness to commit the crime, and for that reason is a more serious modality of typical conduct than is eventual malice.

For its part, culpable crime (article 18, II) is a different form of culpability than malicious crime. In culpable crime, the definition is due to action of presumable behavior that is prohibited by law, even if the author did not desire to accomplish the illegal result. Guilt, in this way, comes about through imprudence (risky, daring conduct), negligence (careless conduct), or ineptitude (conduct without skill or capacity), characterizing violation of an objective duty in action, care or diligence.

It is exactly as a result of this verification that, with each guilty person, the State must assume its constitutional obligation of sufficiently justifying use of a penalty, a powerful instrument of coercion for limiting individual rights, with the purpose of assuring harmonious coexistence in society, mainly because of the occurrence of perverse crimes that annihilate defenseless victims and leave a mark of human tragedy in history.

The world cannot forget, for example, that obstinate determination to change personal genetic characteristics brought about one of the most morbid chapters of the Nazi regime during World War II. The Head of the Medical Department in the Auschwitz Concentration Camp in Germany, Josef Mengele, became notorious for experiments in the area of generic manipulation, which he carried out on children, twins, dwarfs and pregnant women, with a delirious scientific objective. He sought to change hair color and injected dyes to turn eye color to blue. He applied cement injections into women's uteruses and loved castrating young Jews, performing operations without anesthesia and treatments using gasoline, phenol and acid. The Objective: reproduce in the laboratory the Aryan race (predominantly blond and blue-eyed), which, due to its superiority, was the only race deserving the gift of life. Mengele, the "Angel of Death," was accused of practicing crimes against humanity (ordering the mutilating and death of some 400,000 persons), but curiously, took a daily stroll through the Auschwitz camp, warbling and whistling Wagner and Mozart compositions (Manvell & Frankel, 1968, pp. 143-145).

Another tragic record of defenseless victims is reported by the noted Russian author Aleksander Soljenitzyn.

In his notable work of literature, *The Gulag Archipelago,* Aleksander Soljenitzyn impressively relates the painful consequences imposed on all Russian citizens, who, after establishment of revolutionary power in 1917, in the Soviet Union, dared to combat the Bolshevik Party regime. The blacklists sent by the Party directors at the slightest suspect, a report from a secret agent or even an anonymous tip were enough to lead to prison and to inevitable accusation with terrible threats and all manner of tortures in summary proceedings.

Soljenitzyn recalls automobile headlights to "illuminate" the accused; air condition that alternately put out cold and fetid air, tickling a prisoner's nose with a feather, the act of putting out cigarettes on the prisoner's skin, strong electric light in a small cubicle with white walls, sleep deprivation, instruments that smashed nails, the female investigator who performed a strip-tease during interrogations to embarrass the accused, the dungeons where an imprisoned man, naked or only in his underwear was enfeebled by hunger and cold (Soljenitzyn, 1973, pp. 107-124).

To sum it up, all of the perverse methods we have just described, leave us to meditate, appalled, upon the tragic paths traveled because of human cruelty and insensateness. Besides offending human physical integrity and dignity, they degrade the sense and majesty of justice, through the inspiration of feelings and acts of implacable terror, which make it impossible to defend the offended person.

On the other hand, there is not doubt that in certain concrete situations, along with the author of the crime, the victim may not be defenseless or may not deserve recognition of his or her innocence, when for any reason she or he may become a *programming victim*, in a manner of speaking, and may, in certain circumstances, reveal a nature of special inclination or tendency towards a victimal state (latent victim) or towards active delinquency (delinquent due to tendency).

Here one may see the basis for *victimal culpability*, when someone proceeds with malice or guilt, establishing the link between the censurable conduct and the event in the following occurrences:

Programming victim. When the victim sets up the arrangement that leads to a criminal action, assuming a clear role as actor, sometimes in an extraordinarily complex environment that sets in motion the crime that he or she has programmed, providing the means for involving a certain level of culpability, malicious or willful, for the person who is later accused as author of the crime.

Precipitating victim. When the victim joins or supports the action, contributing on some manner, with malice or guilt, to the action or omission of the offender in the process of executing or consummating the crime. As the French say *"la victime éveille l'apetit"* (the victim arouses the appetite), that is, becomes bait for the aggressor.

Forms of expressing the victim's *programming* or *precipitating,* according to the description of the typical conduct set in motion in a concrete case, are:

a. *Exclusively guilty victim.* This would be in a circumstance where the victim's conduct impedes the formation of a causal link that would justify an author's objective liability, with the resulting disappearance of the judicial reasons that could condemn the author under the limits of criminal justice, require him or her to make restitution under Civil Law, or impose any other sanction under some sort of administrative procedure.

b. *Concurrent guilty victim.* This happens when there is intervention through the victim's conduct, which contributes towards subjective plurality characterized during execution of the infraction perpetrated by the author. This would be the case of concurrent liability in a banking establishment, which has the duty of indemnifying an account holder for pain and suffering because it made payment on a false or adulterated check.

c. *Reciprocally guilty victim.* He or she has a certain degree of liability because of a lack of caution and diligence in a given victimogenous situation. This would be the case with an account holder who facilitates, by omission, access to his or her checkbook that was used in falsification.

We should reaffirm, that, with the recognition of victimal culpability, in the case of programming or precipitating the crime, one may detect the nature of a special inclination towards a victimal state (latent victim) or towards active delinquency (delinquent due to tendency).

On the other hand, one must also note two distinct categories of *victimal eventuality,* known as cases of *acts of God* or *casus major*, which may compel the victim's conduct in a certain direction, without there being, however, a crime to be punish due to lack of typical conduct.

a. *Victim due to act of God.* This involves a person who suffers because of a phenomenon of nature or a calamity dictated by chance, when he or she is faced with a given fact that goes beyond the limits of human caution and the normal possibilities of prediction or predictability, which is the capacity or aptitude for foreseeing an occurrence. It is as if something walking down the street is struck by a lightning bolt, or, in another possibility, the disaster befalling a driver who becomes a victim when the seal connected to the steering wheel of the vehicle he or she is driving is broken. There is no crime to be punished, because there is no typical conduct due to malice or guilt.

b. *Victim of casus major.* In *casus major*, the person, without conditions for offering resistance, suffers from the effects resulting from pressure that is greater than the limits of his or her will and of behavior suggested by the moral sense. This would be the case of irresistible coercion that removes a person's psychic or physical freedom of exercising the will and free determination, such as in extreme situations in which she or he is seeking to guarantee survival, or in cases of clinical disturbances such as sleepwalking and hypnotically induced trance. There is no crime to be punished, because no typical conduct due to malice or guilt can be verified as being part of the act.

Acts of God and *casus major* require a supplementary explanation.

In penal dogmatics, the predominant thinking is in favor of the theory of objective imputation, in the sense that *acts of God* and *casus major* are factors that do not result in configuration of a criminal act, exactly because of the absence of malicious or culpable conduct. It is thus inferred that the interference of one of those factors (*act of God* or *casus major*) excludes culpability, related to the event, which was not motivated by the subject's intentions.

One must note, however, that *act of God* and *casus major* do not erase a possible characterization of the causal link, in the line that unfolds action going from human behavior to production of a result.

In relation to an *act of God,* on cannot deny, for example, this relation of causality, in the circumstance of a driver surprised by the rupture in brake pressure in his or her car brakes, leading to collision with a lamp post and the death of a pedestrian. In this case, a causal link is applicable, because had the driver not been driving the vehicle, the accident would not have occurred. What is excluded is recognition of human activity involving malice or guilt, considering that the behavior is atypical, and, since there is no infraction of conduct, obviously no value judgment will be issued on illicitness and culpability.

The same reasoning is juxtaposed in the use of *casus major*, as happened in the hinterland of the State of Bahia, Brazil, when the head of a family, fleeing from drought, who after having given his children all of the water they had, overcome by thirst and without any other option, uncontrollably drank all of the cane rum in his canteen. Drunk, he lost control over his reflexes and, in a state of disorientation, wounded a friend with a knife. The relation of causality is relevant, since, had he not avidly consumed the alcoholic drink, he would certainly not have inflicted bodily harm on his traveling companion.

VICTIMAL CULPABILITY

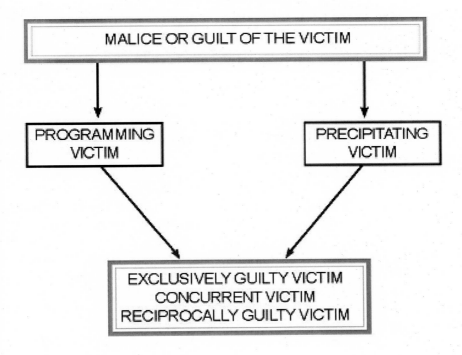

TYPICAL CONDUCT

MALICE OR GUILT OF THE VICTIM

PROGRAMMING VICTIM

PRECIPITATING VICTIM

EXCLUSIVELY GUILTY VICTIM
CONCURRENT VICTIM
RECIPROCALLY GUILTY VICTIM

VICTIMAL EVENTUALITY

ACT OF GOD VICTIM

CASUS MAJOR VICTIM

In light of all of this, we may say that, to the same extent that the criminal models his or her victim, the latter can model the criminal through programming or through precipitation, be it with awareness of her or his conduct and result, be it through not observing the necessary care that was objectively predictable, but not avoided, because the victim slipped up and passed the threshold of critical sensibility, without being aware of the danger ahead. As a result, an inevitable event occurs, which must be investigated to learn the level of greater or lesser collaboration that the victim provides for the action or omission of the person who, operating as author or participant, employs physical, moral or intellectual action, in producing damages characterized by harm or danger to the victim.

In fact, it is perceivable today, in the field of applying Criminal Justice that one of the most dynamic areas in modern victimology is in investigations related to of the deviance that expresses a direct relationship between victim and offender. In terms of criminal dogmatics those studies are extremely important, because they allow not only the individualization of the delinquent, but also individualization of the victim under broader and better defined criteria, in the sense of offering the *arbitrium judicis* a varied range of information capable of recommending the acknowledgment of innocence or of the type of sanction that corresponds to the degree of culpability.

It is exactly due to those factors, Heitor Piedade Júnior points out (1993, pp. 107-115) that the norms derived from Victimology are being frequently observed in several cases being investigated in the sphere of formal levels of control—Police and Justice—where victimological examination is becoming significantly important as a means for multidimensional observation of the victim, involving a broad study of personal, family and social background, as well as for obtaining data linking the scale of the person's intervention or participation in the workings of the crime.[1]

We now move to identifying victimal culpability in the diversified involvement of his or her typical conduct in the criminal phenomenon.

The hypotheses are *victim precipitated or programmed crime*.

Medical Actions

In a monograph this author wrote about stimuli by the victim for practicing delinquent actions (Oliveira, 1998, p. 16), specifically in the field that may involve action by medical professionals, I highlighted the hypothesis of recognizing personalities who produce conditions for being harmed, either through the influence of disturbances in the central nervous system caused by neurosis, or by perturbation due to depression, which can lead to depression. This being the case, human nature in those circumstances makes use of the shelter provided by Medical Science to compensate for the sentiment of unconscious guilt, creating an environment not only for office visits, examinations and surgeries, but even for scientific experiments, transforming the doctor into an instrument of predisposition towards victimicy (Coleman, 1973, pp. 204-205). The patient, in a state of searching, going beyond what the doctor can offer, finds an alternative for conflicts or frailties, unconsciously engendering a purpose of self-punishment, supported by the technical collaboration provided by the Medical professional. The doctor then, is the *"ideal key"* for fitting into the *"problem keyhole,"* represented by the victim's own existential situation.

One may illustrate this conjecture by remembering the typical symptoms of *Body Dysmorphic Disorder* (BDD, the new psychiatric classification for *self-image* problems in the category of *Morphophobia*, that is, fear of one's own shape, known in the United States as *"Mirror Syndrome."* For someone with BDD, plastic surgery may represent relief from depression or Anguish, when it leads to aesthetic reform of some part of the patient's body, which actually develops an inner drama with emotional issues that would be better resolved through *Psychotherapy,* and not *Plastic Surgery.*

This is the perfect hypothesis of a **victim due to latency or tendency**, which we described in the chapter on the historical importance of Victimology. This would be a person who, due to endogenous conflicts or mesological influence, displays a special disposition or inclination towards antisocial conduct, and thus has a greater than normal propensity for being affected by certain forms of victimization, without dispensing with the route of seducing or impelling the offender to be exposed or to plunge into the purpose of the crime.

With regard to a focus on Victimology, it is also relevant to highlight the criminogenous role that the doctor may represent in two other distinct hypotheses.

The first concerns a doctor who, in interacting with the patient, manifests a certain dose of aggression and senselessness, increasing the suffering of someone who needs comfort and support. Cases have been reported of medical professionals who derive a morbid pleasure from observing the suffering of a victim, and even in seeing him or her die, as can be seen from the enormous repercussions of the news story from 1995 in the United States, involving the medical pathologist Jack Kevorkian, nicknamed **Doctor Death**, accused by the American Medical Association of being an enthusiastic defender of *euthanasia* and *assisted suicide*. It should be remembered that euthanasia should not be confused with assisted suicide. *Euthanasia* is death motivated by mercy or compassion that someone provides for another to end unbearable suffering resulting from an incurable or irreversible disease. A terminological variation on euthanasia is *orthonasia*, or passive euthanasia, which consists of omitting or suppressing medical-scientific measures that might temporarily prolong the life of a patient, already kept alive by instruments in a merely artificial state. For its part, *assisted suicide* occurs when a person, submerged in profound suffering, takes the initiative of requesting interference or help from someone in committing suicide.

Doctor Death was accused of helping some 130 of his terminal patients end their lives by means of a suicide machine, a device created by Jack Kevorkian himself, in which one need merely press a button to receive a lethal injection of substances containing the drug Thiopental and potassium chloride, which accelerate death. In April 1999, in the city of Pontiac, Michigan, Jack Kevorkian was finally convicted for the death of Thomas Youk, who was suffering from an incurable degenerative disease.

The second hypothesis, in which the doctor can prepare the coordinates for his or own victimization, is possible in the case of a patient who becomes outraged to learn that he or she is paying to be a victim, when the doctor, to obtain undue profits or advantages, engenders a treatment with fraudulent means, sometimes even with forced hospitalization and surgical intervention. As a result, there is a sharp reaction and repulsion by the patient and her or his family against the criminogenous self-blame by the doctor, who may, in fact, be criminally prosecuted for fraud (article 171 of the Penal Code) and for the practice of kidnapping and private imprisonment (article 148 of the Penal Code).

All of these explanations corroborate the convincing doctrine of professor Jorge de Figueiredo Dias (1993, p. 246), in showing "how very important **victimological investigations** are for the effective application of Criminal Law, in the dynamic process of verifying criminal responsibility, and, consequently, in defining the penalty measure." There is no doubt that, in cases involving investigation of medical error, an analysis of the victim's behavior can play a relevant or even decisive role for faithful elucidation of facts involving the occurrence and explanation of the complex criminal phenomenon.

Elimination of Life: Homicide, Euthanasia, Suicide and Assisted Suicide

When investigating assassinations in Philadelphia in 1956, professor Marvin Wolfgang analyzed around 588 cases of homicide, reaching the conclusion that 26% of the cases analyzed would fit into the category of *homicide precipitated by the victim,* since these were clear circumstances in which the victim was the first to show or use a lethal weapon, strike the first blow during an argument, the first one to begin the march of physical violence. Professor Wolfgang (1957, p. 10) inferred that in such particularities homicides occurred predominantly among people who coexisted in a family, social or professional relationship, and additionally, exhibited characteristics compatible with the attitudes of a delinquent.[2] Research carried out later, involving in the same way investigation of homicides precipitated by the victims, generated similar conclusions in other excellent study centers in the United States, such as the Universities of Chicago and New York (Pokorny, 1965, pp. 479-480); Göppinger, 1975, p. 367).

Given the complex phases of maturation that a crime normally passes through from cogitation to consummation, very frequently a homicide in a fit of passion reveals a percentage of culpability on the part of the victim in setting up or molding his or her own victimization, attracting the aggressor as sheep attract wolves in the field. Consequently, the sentiment of repulsion that leads to someone exterminating the object of passion derives from a profound disturbance of the emotions that impedes self-control and leads to despair (Jímenez de Asúa, 1961, pp. 26-27). It is exactly in this state of intense emotion that the crime takes place, transforming love into a criminogenous factor motivated by anguish, which, for its part, feeds hatred or vengefulness against the loved one or against a real or imaginary rival.[3] This happens in the outcome of certain amorous involvements affected by exacerbation of insane passions that are deeply marked by a possessive, blind and insecure love, and that as a rule serve as a bridge for crimes and fatal tragedies.

Also regarding victim precipitation in the set of situations involving elimination of life, the German psychoanalyst Karl Menninger wrote a worked entitled *Man Against Himself* (Seeling, 1956, pp. 92-93), in which he focused on analyzing personalities who seek suicide, moving in the direction of opportunities for death, stimulated by the unconscious dynamization of their serious conflicts,[4] humiliation,[5] or because of being subjected to unbearable living conditions.[6] Referring to the concrete or potential ties that link the victim to the aggressor in illicitness, Pietro Nuvolone of Italy presented the following considerations: "the motivation for the criminal act can in fact arise from entirely licit and socially admissible relations between the active subject and the passive subject, although from those relations may arise abnormal situations, which can even reach the state of mental illness, and which, in practice, constitute the motive for the crime. Let us reflect, for example, on homicides committed with the consent of the offended subject, which would be the hypotheses of: a) suicide pact; b) suicide by another's hand or assisted suicide; c) collective suicide, as in the case of cult members; d) euthanasia; e) homicides and suicides caused by jealousy, in which one of the persons kills him or herself and then commits suicide, so that both can free themselves from states of anguish that they consider unbearable." (Nuvolone, 1975, p. 50).

On the other hand, it is obvious that in the tumultuous world we inhabit nowadays, in which drug use and abuse are commonly related to the value, on a greater or lesser scale, that the person attributes to his or her human existence. In this regard, Wolf Middendorf (1973, pp. 119-127) says that the weakness of not being able to bear the pain of survival, joined with evaluation of affection or self-esteem, can lead the depressed person to plunge into the disquieting process of suicide brought about by drug consumption.

Another form of suicide that receives much comment in Victimological research refers to wrongs by negligence, especially those caused by traffic accidents. Josefina Ríos Mendoza (1953, p. 43) made an in-depth study into these acts of wrongful negligence and observed the workings of psychological factors and temperamental difficulties that are translated into lack of attention, recklessness, rage, anguish, fear, etc. They thus contribute to the dynamics of the misfortune, enabling suicide, and additionally, bringing the risk of injuries or death to persons who have nothing to do with the problem that generated the occurrence.

In this manner a personality contaminated by a physical or mental drama may be victimized by supporting issues. And thus some people even reach the point of being potential risk factors, as in episodes that accentuate the tendency or arouse impulsiveness towards homicide, suicide, assisted suicide or euthanasia.

Diagnosis of potential risk factors may be verified in one of the symptoms of depression, known as sickness of the soul, that has harmed or destroyed years of useful life amongst the population as a whole. Here are some of the symptoms of depression listed in Psychiatry:

a. recurring idea of suicide or death;
b. end of a love relationship;
c. lack of interest in life;
d. absence of a loved one;
e. lack of perspectives for the future;
f. excessive expectations with regard to something;
g. incapacity of avoiding loss or abandonment;
h. financial problems;
i. feeling of emptiness or uselessness;
j. reduced self-esteem;
k. intense rage or hatred;
l. guilt feeling;
m. intense pains
n. chronic or incurable disease;
o. excessive consumption of alcohol or drugs.

Physical Harm (Assault and Battery) and Torture

As to the appearance of crimes of assault and battery and torture, in harmony with the concept of victim-precipitation, the victimal state, in these cases, presents the same characteristics that accompany homicide, assisted suicide or euthanasia, being distinguished only, obviously, by the effects of the damages caused to health or physical or psychic integrity of the victimized person. The death event may, in fact, result, due to the physical offenses inflicted.

In mentioning the cases of assault and battery and torture, Mendelsohn alluded to the existence of "certain individuals who stand out because of the fact that they expose themselves to accidents with unusual frequency, creating conditions that are propitious for their being harmed or attacked." (Quinney, 1972, pp. 59-60

Von Henting notes that crimes of assault and battery and torture are among the most illustrative manifestations that show when "offender and victim fit with each other as a keyhole and a key." (Mendelsohn, 1981, pp. 59-60).

Examples of the three situations:

a.   a wife repeatedly tortured by her husband;
b.   the domestic tyrant who constantly mistreats his children, in episodes in which this tyrant is reduced to being a victim, when in some way he brings about a reaction of the children in refusing to submit to more punishment;
c.   the employer who imposes humiliations on employees or servants, during day-to-day professional activities.

Extending this reasoning, we may remember victimological behaviors subject to conjugating sadism with masochism and other experiences lived through by the victim, especially when demonstrating the purpose of punishing him or herself personally or with the help of a third party. One sees this in circumstances in which certain people always imagine they have health problems, and thus seek shelter in Medicine, sometimes even creating an environment for performance of dangerous surgical interventions, transforming the doctors into unconscious instruments of those predispositions for victimacy (Henting, 1962, p. 287)

Traffic Accidents

When one interprets a traffic accident one question inevitably is raised: was someone guilty or was it a chance accident?

In the context of these occurrences one frequently finds that, even in small details indications arise as to whom one should attribute the fault: the author or the victim.

Regarding traffic accidents, one generally hears:

- "the driver was not able to brake in time;"
- "the driver was speeding too much;"
- "the driver tried to pass another car;"
- "the pedestrian walked in front of the car;"
- "the pedestrian crossed the street without looking;"
- "the pedestrian did not pay attention at the intersection;"
- "the pedestrian threw him or herself to his or her death."

From a human point of view such inferences are quite understandable, even when they project responsibility for the accident onto the victim, either for having acted with provocation (provoking victim), be it through voluntary exposure (voluntary victim), be it as a result of unconscious problems that lead to lack of personal control (unconscious victim). Those typologies have been minutely examined by Robert Silverman (1997, pp. 55-57).

The **provoking victim** assumes the attitude of creating a propitious situation or of inciting the author to commit the infraction. The **voluntary victim** allows the infraction to be committed, facilitating, aiding or at least not passively offering any resistance. The **unconscious victim** determines the accident due to the lack of attention, care or self-control. The **unconscious victim** may act with *negative guilt* or with *positive guilt*. He or she acts with *negative guilt* by omitting action due to the absence of precaution or to indifference in relation to the act practiced. She or he acts with *positive guilt*, when practicing an act or taking a position in some circumstance in which he or she should not have become involved.

Sexual Intolerance

The role played by the victim in sexual crimes has been the object of repeated debates in the Courts, especially concerning matters of evidence for identifying both the stereotype of innocent victims, attacked through irresistible physical or moral force, and occurrences in which the victim's own attitude opens the door for victimization by arousing the author's imaginative plexus. In this category would be types of rape, sexual harassment and sadomasochism.

Alfred Kinsey dedicated attention to the theme and his research led him to the conclusion that sexual deviancy, especially that which is practiced with minors, tends to occur among people who are particularly close, explaining the attraction of victim by partner, which would be part of the explanation for why some women when under the age of consent have sexual experiences with adult men, preferably relatives or friends, above all when they do not control that which, in modern Psychology, is called *sexual compulsion* (Coleman, 1973, pp. 204-215).

The effect of complicity or voluntary adhesion is a distinctive that frequently stands out in sexual practice initiatives, which for exactly this singularity, should not mean characterizing such acts as sexual wrongdoing.

A brief look at sexuality among indigenous peoples in the Brazilian Amazon serves to justify the reasoning that one should not confuse complicity or voluntary adhesion with the coercion that generates sexual wrongdoing.

The custom of an Indian girl being promised by her parents to a man since childhood, does not mean that she must marry as a virgin. There are records of occurrences where the Indian girl had carnal knowledge even before marriage. On the other hand, while he awaits the moment for marrying the promised bride, the young man practices sexual acts with older women in the village who are not in a marriage commitment, and who thus teach the youths the art of sex.

Seduction, in the sense of deflowering a young girl so that she has carnal knowledge for the first time, without violence or threat, occurs frequently among Amazonian Indians, although it does not constitute a criminal act (Gonzaga, 1972, pp. 38-40). There are several reports of parents who offered their daughters for sexual relations, in exchange for utensils and gifts brought by white men who were passing through the village. Certain tribes also cultivated the custom of the village chief offering a daughter or a sister to be someone's traveling companion, and the person receiving the offer could not refuse without committing an offense. In the same way, an enemy captured in a war between tribes was offered a woman to serve him sexually until the moment when he received the death penalty.

Among Amazonian Indians, extramarital sexual practices are permitted at certain moments. This is the case of the ritual known as *Paiaô,* which exists among the Kayapo nation. According to this ritual, several Indians choose and take an adult woman into the forest, and there have sexual relations with her. But the Kayapo do not accept the practice of carnal knowledge by violence against the woman, nor do they allow a woman to betray her husband. It is said that in the past, a cuckolded husband would kill his rival, roast his body and give the meat for the unfaithful wife to eat. There are no longer any reports of this type of vengeance in modern times (Lukesch, 1976, pp. 268-269).

Menachen Amir was another student of victim-precipitated crime in the area of sexual wrongdoing. He analyzed 646 cases of rape recorded by Philadelphia police in Philadelphia in the United States, which occurred from 1958 to 1960. Fifty-three percent of those cases were practices by individuals who had close ties to the victims, but only 19% could be shown to have been facilitated by the victims. Amir warns of the need to clearly identify the occasions where the victim reacts with determination to the violence or threat,[7] in a clear demonstration of repudiation, since many times resistance serves only for her to simulate that she did not immediately give in to the author's suggestion.[8]

It is appropriate her to call attention to a special concrete case of "violence in a case of the crime of statutory rape," taken up by the Brazilian Supreme Tribunal, when it issued a *Habeas Corpus* to acquit the accused of the charges brought by the Public Prosecution Service.

Here is the argument, supported by Jurisprudence in the vote of the illustrious Justice Marco Aurélio de Mello:

In terms of merit, it is known that in rape crimes, the victim's testimony is undeniably important. In the case in the records, head in Court, she clarified that she had been going out with the patient on his motorcycle, always going to deserted places to exchange kisses and caresses. She noted that she had done the same thing with one of the friends of the accused and with other young men. She also informed that the accused kindly asked her to maintain sexual relations with him, and that she refused, to begin with, but gave in because of the caresses received. Returning to her residence, she asked the patient to leave her far from her house, seeking to escape her father's attention, but, due to bad luck, he saw her getting off of the motorcycle. All indications are that the criminal lawsuit that condemned the accused arose solely and exclusively from the reaction of the victim's father.

In light of these considerations, it must be concluded that the intent of article 213 of the Penal Code, which defines rape as the act of constraining a woman to have carnal knowledge by means of violence or serious threat. The young age of the victim is not something that will remove what she confessed in court, that is, that she maintained relations with the accused of her own free will. The situation becomes really shocking when it is seen that the minor, only twelve years old, was leading a promiscuous life, which corroborates what the Defense presented about her appearance being that of someone older than age twelve.

The presumption of violence provided for in Article 224 of the Penal Code must give way to reality. One cannot refuse to recognize the modification of customs that has been occurring, with frightening speed, over the last few decades. The mass communications media in general, and television in particular, are responsible for mass dissemination of information, which is not even selected according to median and healthy criteria that would meet the minimum requirements of a society marked by dissimilarities. Thus it happens, that given unrestricted access to the media, it is not uncommon to note the precocity with which children today deal without embarrassment with issues concerned with sexuality, in a spontaneous, almost natural manner. This would not be said during the 1940s, the period of the glorious appearance, as a symbol of modernity and liberalism, of our venerable and still binding Penal Code. At that time, a person twelve years of age was in fact considered a child, and, as such, defenseless and unprepared for the traumas of life.

Now, after the passing of more than fifty years—and what years, since, in our view, in the history of humanity they correspond to several well-lived centuries—one cannot equate, since that is absolutely unconceivable, the two situations. In our days there are no children, but twelve year-old maidens. Precociously matured, most of them already have enough discernment to react to eventual adversities, even if they do not yet have a defined set of values, to the point of being able to see all manner of circumstances that may befall them. Such lucidity will in fact only come with time, even if the massacre of mass-produced news, imposed by a media that considers itself omniscient—and many times is known to be irresponsible when faced with the social role that is its duty—leads to precipitation of events that are only welcome with time, that inseparable friend of wisdom.

Therefore, it can be seen that society is no longer aided by the rigors of an outdated, anachronistic Code, which, in some parts is even irrelevant, because it has not kept up with the behavioral revolution witnessed by those who are older. Certainly, the concept of freedom is as discrepant as that of yesterday, which would only be compared to those that in ancient times undergirded the notion of libertinism, anarchy, cynicism and shamelessness.

In the end, a question is appropriate that is so obvious as to seem unnecessary at first sight, even though it has not yet been duly answered: society ages; do not laws also?

Now, since legislation has become stiffened—and laws, instead of clouding the evolution of customs, should accompany and thus protect it— the interpreter of laws has the role of cooling such austerity, making the normative text more flexible from a literal angle, thus making it more adequate and opportune. Otherwise, the argument of security will transform into sophistry, and serve the inexorable despotism of professional archconservatives, in a society that wishes to be global, agile and technologically, socially and spiritually advanced.

At any rate, the heart of the matter is constraint, and in the sense that the victim made it abundantly clear that she had maintained sexual relations spontaneously, one cannot, even by appealing to the age issue, conclude that constraint took place. The presumption is not absolute, and, in this case, it yields to the peculiarities already pointed out, that is, the fact of the victim appearing to be older, leading a dissolute life, going out at all hours of the night and maintaining sexual relations with other youths, as was recognized in the deposition and was public knowledge.

For these reasons, I grant the order to acquit the patient.
That is my vote.

> Marco Aurélio de Mello
> Minister of the Supreme Federal Tribunal
> May, 1996—HC number 73.662-9/MG

In support of the jurisprudential decision we have just mentioned, it is possible to formulate the inference that, in a given circumstance, the victim manifests any sort of *signal,* demonstrating that she would not resist persistence or constraint created by the author in his purpose of sexual harassment. The contact with charm that inflates the ego of the person subjected to the attentions, smooth talking, flattery and the elegant use of seduction are initial procedures in sexual attraction, in conditions of finally leading to conquest of the victim (Menachen, 1967, p. 493).

Under those hypotheses, the victim's conduct indicates a positive expression, such as going to a bar or to a private apartment, or assumes a negative sense, without reacting with sufficient conviction to certain calls, attracted, for example, by the promise of a lucrative job or prosperous career. This is the attitude of someone who exposes the body, with the intent of preferably attracting the attention of someone chosen as a target, using clothes that are considered provocative and sensual in our culture. Exposure, with insinuations showing forms of bodily expression is, when one thinks about it, more and more frequent on the erotic websites that motivate internet users to navigate in search of *virtual sex* promoted through the exhibition of intimacy on internet pages. This shows how the game of seduction, for some, has become more interesting and directly related to social demands, a circumstance with which some people coexist, possibly carrying conflicting sentiments.[9] Many of those are associated with disturbances that make it impossible to control the *obsession-compulsion,* which is capable of leading someone to assume standardized and even repetitive behaviors, giving in to inappropriate perverted impulses[10] to unload intolerable tension.

Theft, Robbery and Abduction

Scientific research in the field of Victimology, even in the sense of gaining a better understanding of the criminal, has served to demonstrate that certain persons are dangerous to themselves and are living vulnerable lives, because, from time to time they take false steps and find themselves face to face with criminality, either through a character given to ostentation, lechery and unfettered living, or because of an excess of carelessness, negligence or imprudent behavior.

Belgian professor Paul Cornil has emphasized that lack of attention regarding material goods can function as a victim-impellent factor, which drives the person into undergoing a victimal situation given the absence of mechanisms for protecting his or her patrimony (Cornil, 1959).

An unconscious or subconscious attitude can certainly stereotype itself through little attention, lack of zeal and care that a person, in a social environment, exhibits in relation to his or her habits, customs, material goods and personal objects. It is evident that this leads the person to act in ways that are sometimes highly risky and create opportunities that facilitate maneuvers by authors who are specialized in practicing crimes against patrimony, notably in large urban centers, with their routines of social intranquility provided by **pickpockets, delinquent children, robbers** and **kidnappers** who avidly seek to extort economic advantage, even if by means of threats, physical mutilation or death of the victim.

Related to this, regarding the unconscious or subconscious contribution that the victim is capable of providing to a criminal activity, Italian professor Benigno Di Tullio has divided victimogenous factors into **victim-impellent** and **victim repellent.** While **victim-impellent** factors drive the person towards experiencing a victimal situation, the victim **repellent** factors inhibit or impede such a situation. The **victim-impellent** and **victim repellent** factors can act simultaneously, as happens with the millionaire who is always running the risk of being robbed or kidnapped, but nonetheless employs protective measures and mechanisms to keep at bay those who would wish to make such a favored person a victim (Di Tullio, 1963, pp. 96-97).

Using Di Tullio's ideas as a basis, crimes against patrimony involve a technical configuration of **unleashing victimogenous factors**, as a result of their nature that facilitates crime or exposes the victim to it, as can be seen in the following specific behaviors:

a. parking a car with an improperly locked door or key in the ignition;
b. leaving the car forgetting objects that may attract attention inside;
c. stopping the car at a traffic light, holding one's arm outside with a watch clearly in sight;
d. driving along dark streets in deserted areas;
e. being with a boyfriend or girlfriend in a deserted or suspicious place;
f. patronizing promiscuous environments;
g. traveling through dangerous neighborhoods;
h. displaying, without discretion, jewelry or valuable objects;
i. deliberately displaying large amounts of money;
j. leaving purses, wallets, bags and packages unprotected on trips;
k. leaving doors or windows open when leaving one's residence;
l. giving interviews related to the fortune one owns;
m. showing one's luxurious house in magazines, newspapers, on television or the internet.

Fraudulent Maneuvers

Another type of crime where victim-precipitation is common involves fraud and different ways of deceiving one's neighbor with a *mise en scène* to fool people and obtain illicit profits. In this area of fraudulent maneuvers, Willy Callewaert, in France, conceived the thesis of "victim due to one's own dishonesty" (Callewaert, 1959, pp. 613-614), one who does not try to note the offender's artifices and snares, because he or she also has expectations of dishonest gain, having been contaminated by bad faith and greed.

In swindles, there is frequently a noteworthy interaction between the active subject and the passive subject. In this crime and in other forms of fraud, at first sight, one thinks that the victim is perfectly innocent, but, as the case is investigated, one may find a certain degree of culpability

on the part of the victim, who allowed him or herself to be taking in by
the swindler's art in skillfully playing on her or his dishonest instincts,
which may express an unconscious desire to allow oneself to be de-
frauded, attracted by the bait of profit rapidly obtained by fraudulent
means (Callewaert, 1959, pp. 615). These actions involve techniques
that arouse the victim's appetite so as to be, at the appropriate moment
"cut down on his own ground" (Andrade, 1980), p. 191-193). That is
how *bilateral fraud* happens, when the victim him or herself suffers
damage because she or he was not able to succeed with a criminal intention. Neither of the two is innocent, not the author, not the victim, because both want an illicit end, in their *modus operandi*, with mutual
deception. This would be a case of bilateral turpitude in the *guitar confidence tale*, in which the victim intends to gain an advantage in manufacturing counterfeit money by acquiring forbidden machinery.

We may cite other examples:

a.   purchase of a false winning lottery ticket;
b.   obtaining false honorary titles or academic degrees;
c.   victim of matrimonial fraud who turns a wealthy patrimony
     over to a conniving spouse;
d.   package confidence game.

What does the *package money confidence game* consist of? It gets
this name usually employs a from its use of a package of old paper that
simulates paper money, generally covered with a real note, this package
being used by the swindler who engenders this trickery.

The agent cuts a series of pieces of newspaper, into the exact size of
twenty-dollar bills, makes eight packs of these pieces, giving the impression that there are, say, eight packs of two hundred dollars each. He or
she later takes a twenty-dollar bill and adjusts this bill to the curves of
each pack, wrapping them up and tying them strongly so that, if someone
tears a small part of the wrapping, the edges appear, as if there really
were eight packages of two hundred dollars of each.

Then, this agent walks up to a person at the Bus Station and declares:
"Sir, could you do me a favor? I have these sixteen-hundred dollars to
deliver, to my sister's address in Manhattan, but I have an urgent trip to
Boston. I have to catch my bus now. I can see that you are a person of
good, serious and certainly honest appearance, and so, who knows, could
you maybe do me a favor?" The victim sees the package representing a

fairly high sum and accepts the errand: "Of course, I'll deliver your package." But the agent, before saying goodbye, indicates that he or she has no money. "But sir, could you lend me a hundred dollars? I'll telephone my sister and she will pay you there." The individual is warned not to open the package, because it has to be delivered in full. The agent also adds that the money is for paying a debt, and so no money can be taken from the package. And the victim, *already in bad faith,* thinking he is going to acquire sixteen-hundred dollars, again checks the packages; the appearance is perfect, he is used to dealing with money, and does not hesitate in taking two hundred dollars from his own pocket and handing it do the agent, who boards a bus and disappears. Next, the victim opens the package and sees that he has been fooled. There are only pieces of newspaper, with only one twenty dollar bill.

Seeing that he has been swindled, the victim goes to the Police, complaining that he has fallen for the *package confidence game*, while certainly hiding that his attitude was one of bath faith.

Had he really acted in good faith, he would have delivered the package at the specified address, in Manhattan. By acting with indiscretion in opening the package, it became evident that the victim really intended to keep the money. He ended up losing money.

The swindler normally seeks to create a relationship of confidence with the victim at the outset, transmitting an image of respectability. Later, he or she expresses concern with the victim's problems, providing support, building an alliance, even if it is illusory. It is in this gradual victimization process that the delinquent leads the victim to become malleable and obedient, in a castle of lies built to put the crime into practice.[11] Once the crime has been consummated, the victim encounters reality, and sees that his or her intelligence and personal freedom have been assaulted. There are even cases in which the victim contributes towards impunity for the delinquent in being hindered in communicating the fact to the authorities, preferring to keep silent over what has happened as a result of the perpetrator's scheme, notably when the problem affects the victim's social image.

Corruption and Illicit Enrichment

In defining bribery, corruption is paying or promising something that is not owed to achieve the performance of an official act; being corrupted in accepting an undue patrimonial advantage, as provided for in articles 333 and 317 of the Penal Code.

One can be a victim of oneself in the crime of corruption. The corruptor who attends to a request for undue advantage, made by a public servant, is harmed in the sense of suffering patrimonial loss in paying that which was requested. But this loss should be attributed to him or her, because she or he bore it in order to achieve a desired end.

In several ways and in several degrees someone can become a victim of corruption. This happens first of all, individually, then as participant in a group and, finally, as a member of the population in general.

There are various factors that cause of contribute towards someone becoming a victim of corruption. There are even people carrying within themselves the psychological condition for this. Exaggerated credulity, excessive confidence, ingenuity, confidence, timidity, all of these are psychological factors. Alongside them are factors that are even psychopathic: crepuscular states, distraction, illusions, amnesia, delirium, oligophrenia, apathy, temperament and character disturbances, psychoses and neuroses (Palmieri, 1965, pp. 828-831).

Sometimes the victims are dispersed throughout a community or even in society in general. These are diffused interests that are affected by acts of corruption. The tax evader does not nominally affect one or several persons. The victims are all those who are deprived of enjoying the social advantages brought by positive employment of the money that was withheld. Cartels, dumping, oligopolies, irrational exploitation of mineral resources, industrial pollution, frauds against worker's rights and so many other contrivances that corrupt persons use, harm, victimize, damage and sacrifice the diffuse interests of a larger or smaller number of persons.

There are cases in which the victim is affected by his or her own corruption. This is common in situations of bilateral turpitude, situations in which there is an attempt to take advantage of the aggressor's trick.

It is not rare for the corrupt person to try and anesthetize his or her own conscience and seek to neutralize guilty feelings, through the technique of neutralizing the ethical value of her or his acts, as was emphasized by professor Manoel da Costa Andrade (1980, p. 155). One neutralization technique consists in the corruptor believing that the victim, in some cases more corrupt than he or she, will have an active participation in the crime. In the cases of bilateral turpitude, the affected party may also take advantage of what he or she supposes to be an error by the offender. Another technique is self-suggestion that the victim will not feel the loss, which happens in cases of small swindles on major millionaires. A third technique is for the corrupt person to think of the action as a means of punishing the user, who is exploiting other people's need. There is also the possibility of the corrupt person to try and convince himself or herself that the act is nothing more than an *occulta compensatio,* as in the case of an employee who believes she or he is being exploited by the boss and cheats him or her as a form of attaining compensation. Another factor that neutralizes the corrupt person's scruples is the fact that the victims are often diluted in a crowd and do not feel the damage. Finally, it may happen that the corrupt person will excuse him or herself before her or his own consciousness, trying to believe that the damage done is minimal and will not harm the others.

With corruption there is frequently the hypothesis of sacrificing an undetermined number of victims. This is especially common in "white-collar crime," dealt with for the first time as a doctrine by E. Sutherland (1937, pp. 60-63). In white-collar crimes, the victim enters the aggressor's cogitations only in an impersonal, abstract manner. The author is not targeting specific person, and usually does not even know the victims. Gilbert Geis notes that in many manifestations of *white-collar crime,* precipitation towards the crime occurs with victims whose personalities have characteristics similar to those of the infractors (Geis, 1961, p. 89).

In this way, it is not difficult to detect precipitation by the victim in expressions of criminality that involve corruption and other forms of illicit enrichment in the exercise of a public mandate, position, job or function in public administration. That finding is plausible essentially if we take into account that, the victims appearing in those crimes usually belong to political or economic power elites, who share the same aspirations of the delinquents in terms of expectations to easy gains and rapid accumulation of wealth, albeit in a dishonest manner.

It is opportune to point out that the generalized routine of corruption and illicit enrichment crimes, in their multiple manifestations, with successive scandals reported by the press, has att5racted the attention of students of Victimology to the large incident of **collective victimization** in the structure of society.

Collective victimization is present in the effects that spread, with high social and economic costs, among the members of a community. Public money and the administration of services directed by the State, which should be employed in satisfying the needs of the people, are continuously diverted from their real finalities, producing precarious social wellbeing, tax overloads, raising of tariffs on essential services, shortages of essential consumer products, besides the negative impact on the spirits of honest people who feel violated.

In the commotion of this organized criminality, while the people in general pay more and more dearly for everything, the agents of corruption continue their illicit enrichment, without prosecution and without punishment, covered by privileges that support impunity.

Extortion and Blackmail

The *victim-precipitated crime* model may also appear in events in which the delinquent seeks to receive an undue economic advantage at the cost of constraining someone to do, allow to be done or not do something. In such circumstances, it is very common to have a threat of revealing facts that might compromise the reputation and set of personal qualities that the victim has gathered during the course of a lifetime (Andrade, 1980, p. 187; Sutherland, 1961, p. 230; Shapiro, 1976, p. 60).

Nowadays, the urban centers, especially those that are most developed, are extremely susceptible to favoring blackmail and extortion, since there are frequent opportunities for people to lead forms of social or professional life, sometimes even supported by marketing that exhibits a public image that is not compatible with their own concepts, and in some cases is diametrically opposed to the demands of their private identity.

In the open channels between intimate life and the way a person presents him or herself in social relations, the blackmailer frequently penetrates, coldly making use, as Adolphe Gouldner recorded, "of the dramatic world of appearances, a very thin cover where one must tread carefully, to avoid it breaking and revealing the undesirable (Gouldner, 1873, p. 351). In many cases there is no escape, and the victim is caught in the crossfire of opting for the financial transaction in exchange for the integrity of his or her image, having to bear the conflict between convenience and what might seem to be more worthy and sincere.

Erving Goffman very properly notes that "the victims in those contingencies must necessarily pay a high psychological price, endure a very high level of anxiety for leading a day-to-day life that can collapse at any moment. It is exactly from exploiting that gear that the blackmailer feeds, taking advantage of knowing stigmatizing secrets, which always explodes in atypical situations such as: homosexuality, prostitution, abortion, adultery, gambling, corruption or drug consumption."

It is interesting to note that the crime of blackmail ends up creation a sort of *de facto* solidarity between the delinquent and the victim, as happens with the **victimless crimes** (Goffman, 1976, p. 108). The difference is that in the **victimless crimes**, unlike in blackmail, there are no antagonistic and conflicting relationships. Raymond Garraud summarizes it precisely: "On the day when the blackmail victim wants to denounce the author, he will inflict upon himself the evil of publicity, which, above all, he wishes to avoid."[12] The same reasoning applies in relation to that objective on the part of the delinquent.

Invasion of Individuality and Invasion of Privacy

Human intimacy has been interpreted as a key element for disseminating symptoms of a personality that places in check relations between technological progress and the right of preserving the particularities of the *individual sphere* and the *private sphere* in the life of each person.

Here we open a space for an authoritative lesson from Professor Paulo José da Costa Júnior:

Corresponding to his natural division into an individual being and a social being, man lives as a personality in different spheres, in an *individual sphere* and a *private sphere*.

Therefore, man, as a person, seeks to satisfy fundamental interests: as an individual, interest in a free existence; as a co-participant in the human consortium, interest in a free development in a life of relation.

While the rights destined towards protecting the *individual sphere* serve to preserve the personality within public life, in protecting the *private sphere* one considers the inviolability of the personality within its refuge, necessary for development and evolution, in its own particular world, alongside external life. In this way, the difference between the *individual sphere* (protection of honor) and the *private sphere* (protection against indiscretion) is established.

Looking at the distinction from a psychological angle, one might argue that human behaviors are *open*, when easily perceptible. The are *valued* and *covered,* when not perceptible by their own nature (dreams, fantasies), or when the subject does not expose them to third parties, which can all be combined, or make an exception in the case of a close circle of friends. Covert conduct corresponds to the 'private self,' which travels inside the *individual sphere.*

Interest in the relationship life prevails in the *individual sphere.* Among the most important manifestations of the *individual sphere* are the right to one's name and reputation. The former assures the individual, in the case of abuse by third parties, of his own individuality. The latter allows him to intend to assure social esteem, shielding him from defamatory attacks from fellow citizens.

In counterpoint to this, there is the *individual sphere,* the *particular* or *private sphere.* Here it is no longer a citizen of the world, relating to those who are similar, as in the *individual sphere.* On the contrary, this is the citizen, in intimacy or reserve, in moral isolation, living with his own individuality. (Costa Júnior, 1970, pp. 24-25)

There are people who, consciously or unconsciously, from time to time expose themselves to enormous publicity, without bothering themselves about it, or lacking means to protect themselves from the overwhelming risks projected by the industrial refinements of modern communications instruments: internal television systems, devices for telephone call interception, hidden cameras for photographing, taping or filming and computers.

In focusing on conventional means of communication enhanced by technology, special note should be given to the internet and the press.

The internet today is an enormous field for information about consumer habits, correspondence, consultations, the most varied kinds of research and dissemination of messages about the individuality and privacy of people.

The mechanisms that corrode the frontiers of intimacy, the infringements of private life have become even more disquieting with the advent of the worldwide computer network, exactly because, going beyond the worthy purpose of facilitating comfortable interpersonal communication, the internet has provided a parallel industrialization of vulgarity, with the dissemination of data, photos and details of people, allowing offenses against honor and economic losses with profound repercussions in society.

That being the case, the internet advance brings with it the danger of articulation for wide web of infractions, resulting from *cyber crimes* or *virtual crimes,* which is why there has been increased concern for criminalizing offensive conduct in light of this new reality, which is popularized with the use of devices that offer the ease o mobile internet through cellular telephones and hand-held computers. Regarding the definition of these specific penal types, particularly relevant are: attacks on privacy and intimacy, exploitation of virtual prostitution, obscene publications, pedophilia, corruption of minors, threats, sexual harassment, divulging of secrets, virtual piracy or violation of authorial rights, theft, robbery, frauds, games of chance, offers for drugs, invasion of sites, cyber terrorism, creation and propagation of viruses by hackers, improper appropriation of information or financial values and dissemination of untrue information or concepts. In various actions classified as *virtual crime*, it is not difficult to find a pair formed by an alliance between victim and author, in a criminal pairing that illicitly makes use of the information technology market, in many cases with the participation or connivance of the companies that provide access to the internet. A notable example of that abnormality, as we have emphasized, is that on analyzing the aspects of *violence* and sexual harassment, one finds an increase in the number of erotic sites that motivate internet users to navigate the sexual maze of internet pages.

With regard to action by the press, some aspects deserve distinct consideration.

There is no doubt that the *paparazzi,* the celebrity hunters, have become accustomed to violating individual rights, with the implacable exposure of the intimate life of personages who dominate the fertile terrain of power or seduction. That is why as long as there are surprises caused by scandals, there will be those dedicating themselves to disseminating and selling them, even beyond the parameters of conscience. The law of the market in the press business is the fruit of demands by society itself, in which there is a lack of definition for the boundaries between public and private.

Conjugal crises, love scenes and adulteries are always reflected by the press, especially the sensationalist and vulgar tabloids, which base themselves on the criterion of making public interest prevail, even if the possibility of error can be considerable in evaluating an occurrence that has public transcendence. On the other hand, it is difficult for someone who is a celebrity or star to remain cloistered, especially when it is a question of focusing on the person's intimate life.

Facts and news cannot be transformed into a sacred axiom with the privilege of demolishing human beings and destroying families, even though a public eager to see the ferocity of malicious journalism exists.

The golden mean lies in preserving the moral dosage that the social function of journalist requires of each member of the press. It is not a question of only publishing that which any citizen wants to read, see or hear. Above that aspect, in a process of enhancing personal dignity, the wisdom of the journalistic office must be cultivated, in the sense of measuring how far one may go as a decent professional, without being contaminated by greed and senselessness, which are the leaven for morbid sensationalism.

There is not use having severe laws against invasion of privacy by the press. The question is one of ethical consciousness and that is part of the limits that humans can achieve.

Furthermore, an obvious conclusion can be clearly drawn; many of the celebrities, famous people, who complain about being under heavy fire from photographers and journalists, become victims exactly as a result of complicity with those professionals of the press, because they in some manner are working with them, making secret deals, insinuating or exposing themselves in a purposeful manner to attract opportune publicity that sells because of popular curiosity (Garraud, 1935, p. 260). In contemporary society there is always someone who delights in futility, vulgarity or appearances.

Notes

1. In the Jury Trial of Doca Street, held in the city of Cabo Frio (Rio de Janeiro), in October 1979, the brilliant defense of the experience attorney Evandro Lins e Silva gave a victory to the victimological thesis of effective participation by the victim in hatching the crime. The defense successfully argued that Doca Street had killed his wife Ângela Diniz in defense of his personal dignity, as a consequence of the strong influence of the victim in the unleashing and finishing of the fact, in which provocative attitudes, offenses, confrontation, humiliation and insults directed at the accused were notorious (see Lins e Silva, 1984, pp. 207-211).

2. Among the examples cited by Wolfgang, several would fit the configuration of legitimate defense, such as the provoking father killed by his son with the help of the mother, and the person who tried to practice acts of *sodomy* (non-conventional sexual practice) with a woman, who, in response, refuses and defends herself with a knife, making a victim out of the aggressor.

3. In tragic literature, William Shakespeare's *Othello* describes in stupendous detail the marked distinctions of jealousy and its effects. In the judicial

field, among other excellent works on the theme, one may cite: Théodule Ribot, *Essai sur les Passions* (Paris, 1907); Enrico Ferri, *Os Criminosos na Arte e na Literatura* (Lisbon, 1913); Evaristo de Moraes *Criminalidade Passional* (Rio de Janeiro, 1931); Etienne de Greef, *Amour et Crimes d'Amour* (Brussels, 1942); José Ingenieros, *Tratado del Amor* (Buenos Aires, 1970).

4. Greek Mythology offers us the classic example of the play *Oedipus Rex*, which ends with Jocasta's suicide by hanging, and Oedipus' self-mutilation. According to this tragedy by Sophocles, Oedipus, without knowing, killed his father Laius and married his own mother Jocasta, who bore him three children. Upon discovering he was his father's murderer, the horrified Oedipus put out his own eyes and Jocasta hanged herself. This gave rise to the concept of *Oedipus Complex*, repressed sexual love of the son with regard to his mother.

5. Of the seven Cleopatras recorded in Egyptian history, the last, the one linked to Julius Caesar and Mark Anthony, born in 69 B.C. and died in 30 B.C.—is the most famous, and the one whose agitated life and tragic death has raised the most questions.

We all know about the last moments of the proud queen, who, when abandoned by the good fortune that have accompanied her 39 years of existence, decided to commit suicide so as not to be taken to Rome by Octavius, who wished to display her as a trophy of war.

Most historians state that after shutting herself into her mausoleum, she removed a small venomous serpent from a basket of figs and induced the reptile to bite her on the left breast, the one above the heart.

It is known that Octavius, triumphant over Mark Anthony at Actium (Greece, 31 BC), buried her with full honors next to the tomb of her beloved, as she had requested him before dying.

6. Israel Drapkin (1977, p. 345-350) maintains that delinquents subjected to a prison regime, are always faced with these dramas, because they find themselves victims of the penitentiary system, which, with its pathologies and promiscuity, impedes the social and moral reintegration in the family and community.

7. In an exclusive interview with *Veja* magazine, published in São Paulo on 09/17/1986, journalist and writer Susan Brownmiller, author of the book *Against My Will; Men, Women and Rape* (New York, 1975) declared that during research for her book, in talking with several rapists, many of the delinquents confessed that "sexual violence is nothing more than a stimulating game for the couple. In the beginning the woman says no merely to encourage the author to proceed, and after he has won her, the sex act becomes something marvelous for both of this." This is the drama pointed out by Susan Brownmiller: "passive reaction by the woman during the moment of rape is often confused with pleasure in being dominated."

8. Alfred Kinsey clarifies that the victim may find in the agent someone who represents a successor to her father or a friend. Kinsey carried out these

studies in Philadelphia, in 1954, together with W. Pomeroy, C. Martin and P. Gebhard. The results of their investigations were published as *Sexual Behavior in the Human Female* (Philadelphia, 1953).

9. It is in attitudes of this type that expiation of guilt feelings occurs. Compelled to act with a feeling or sentiment of guilt, the person, involved because of affective conflicts, releases the need to be punished, expresses an attraction for suffering and opens the way for the pleasure of pain. As a result of verification of the crime, the guilt feeling or sensation is relieved with the satisfaction of forbidden impulses, a theme with a great psychoanalytic tradition (Dias & Andrade, 1984, pp. 198-201).

10. The most adequate examples are those learned from the olden times of Mythology. The term **nymphomania** refers to semi-divine mythological beings, the Nymphs, who peopled the forests of the Greco-Roman world, always in search of sexual pleasures. The Roman empress Messalina was a standard for this type of expression of sexuality, since it is said of her that, as well as having a harem of sexual slaves, she had the custom of disguising herself and going out at night around the taverns and streets of ancient Rome, in search of constant and unregulated sexual activities.

11. In French Judicial history, Victor Lusting is remembered as one of the most audacious swindlers, due to his powers of convincement in fooling his victims. Lusting reached the extreme of organizing public auctions to twice sell the Eiffel Tower, the supreme symbol of Paris.

12. Usury is a clear modality of that which, in Criminal Law, is customarily called "victimless crime." The person (victim) functions as a client of the usurer in the in the outworking of that which he or she has in fact unleashed, and even under the humiliations and exorbitance, does not allow her or himself to be oppressed by the sensation of having suffered aggression. In is also possible to identify "victimless crime" in cases of incest, attempted suicide, taking drugs, abortion, etc.

Chapter 10

Victimological Typology: Specific Types of Victims

The Profile of Victimization

In the practical field of Criminal Law, informed by knowledge from Criminology and Victimology, one of the basic concerns must be the methodologically qualified formation of typologies based on observation of human types, in conditions that will be useful in investigating crime, verifying guilt and establishing penal effects, through applying penalties or security measures.

Victimology already has its own typologies that allow one to understand, with a broader scope, the profile of the role performed by the victim in the victimization phenomenon.

Therefore, this book must not fail to adduce the important contributions that indicate multiple classifications of victims formulated by specialists in the area the world over.

Specific Types of Victims

Binyamin Mendelsohn (Israel, 1947)

1. *Completely innocent victim or ideal victim.* This person happens to be uninvolved in the victim's activity, producing nothing and contributing nothing to production of the crime. This would be the case of a woman whose purse is snatched by a thief in the street.

2. *Victim with lessened culpability or through ignorance.* This would be characterized by an involuntary impulse towards wrongdoing. This is

what happens to a couple of lovers have sex in their neighbor's garden, and there are attacked by him because he does not accept their lack of decency. Another example: a woman who performs an abortion on herself using improper means, paying for her ignorance with her life.

3. *Voluntary victim or victim as guilty as the offender.* Anyone can be the criminal or the victim. This happens in cases of a) *Russian Roulette* (only one projectile in the weapon and the contestants spin the drum until one is killed; b) *American Duel* (two weapons, but only one is loaded for the choice).

4. *Victim guiltier than the offender.* May be: a) *Provocative victim,* who incites the author of the crime; b) *Victim due to imprudence,* who causes the accident due to lack of self-control, even though the author bears a share of the blame.

5. *Solely guilty victim.* Classified as: a) *Infracting victim,* who commits and infraction and ends up being the victim, as in the circumstance of homicide in legitimate defense; b) *Simulating victim,* who, due to irresponsible premeditation, leads someone to be accused of a crime, and may cause a serious judicial error; c) *Imaginary victim,* a person with a severe Psychopathic state or other mental disorder, such as Psychosis, Paranoia, Schizophrenia our Neurosis. Someone with a serious mental disturbance has ways of inducing the Courts to error, by posing as a victim of a misdeed, accusing another person of a certain violation without the crime having ever occurred.

Hans von Henting (United States, 1948)

1. *Isolated victim.* Lives alone and does not integrate into the community, thus being exposed to dangerous situations. Examples: the elderly, foreigners, immigrants, widows, deserters, misanthropes.

2. *Victims due to proximity.* These are divided into: a) *Victim due to Spatial Proximity,* who becomes a victim due to being very near the offender in a given place, such as robberies on buses; b) *Victim due to Family Proximity,* generated inside of the family, as happens with parricide, incest and ill-treatment; c) *Victim due to Professional Proximity,* generally evident in professional activities that lead to a closer professional relationship, as occurs with Doctors, Clergy, Lawyers and Dentists.

3. *Victim with desire for profit.* This is someone who, due to the desire for easy or rapid enrichment, falls into the hands of swindlers or confidence artists.

4. *Victim with anxiety for living.* This is a person who, due to not having taken advantage of life so far, tries to make up for lost time and begins to experience greater desire for freedom, and embarks upon adventures, thrills and situations involving risk or danger.

5. *Aggressive victim.* The person becomes this, as a result of suffering aggression up to the breaking point, and reacting to the state of hostility.

6. *Victim of no value.* This is a victim undesired or repudiated by the community, as a result of his or her reprehensible behavior, as happens with a rapist or murderer who ends up being killed by the police or by the victim.

7. *Victim due to emotional state.* Obsession, fear, hatred or feelings of vengeance are examples of emotional states that are propitious for victimization.

8. *Victim due to change in a phase of existence.* The person may become a victim due to some circumstance related to behavioral change at a certain phase in life. It is always said that one must take great care with the passing of childhood to adolescence, adolescence to maturity and maturity to old age. One symptomatic state that is not actually a sexual deviancy, nonetheless brings disquiet to the personality of someone who, beginning at age forty, may become a victim of the *age of the wolf* (called male menopause) or *age of the she-wolf* (called female menopause). In this phase the person, questioning him or herself about her or his sexual life model and physical appearance, may develop a process of lack of self-criticism and exacerbation of the libido with erotic fancies. The fear of old age and the myth of impotence in the *age of the wolf* or *age of the she-wolf*, explain many adolescent attitudes, such as men searching for much younger girlfriends.

9. *Perverse victim.* Here are situated the psychopaths, who may reach the victim state and not be able to establish a limit of respect in regard to other persons, treating them like objects that one manipulates as if in a chess game. This is the case of the *miche,* a male prostitute who empowers his violence and seeks to do away with the life of his gay client, either due to the desire to take goods or objects from or because of feeling betrayed by him.

10. *Alcoholic victim.* Alcohol is among the factors that most create victims, many of them the result of homicide.

11. *Depressive victim.* Intolerable depression can lead to a search for self-destruction, involving the person in an openly victimogenous situation.

12. *Voluntary victim.* This person allows an offense to be committed against him or her, without offering resistance. Many cases appear in sexual situations not involving violence.

13. *Defenseless victim.* This is a person who passes up the chance to prosecute the offender, because judicial prosecution would cause more problems than the suffering resulting from the consequences of the crime. Generally appears in cases of street muggings, sexual violation or blackmail.

14. *False victim.* This is someone who makes him or herself a victim to obtain a benefit, such as claiming insurance or covering a monetary shortfall or robbery.

15. *Immune victim.* This is a person who thinks he or she is not subject to action by anyone to make her or him a victim. Example: Judges and Clergy.

16. *Repeat victim.* This person has already suffered damage and takes no precautions against being victimized again. It is a phenomenon similar to that of a repeat offender.

17. *Victim who becomes an author.* This appears in a process of transmigration of violence. The victim, earlier attacked by the author, prepares a retaliatory strike. Often occurs with war crime.

18. *Victim through propensity.* This person has a propensity towards being a victim. Has a depressed, unfettered, libertine or afflicted personality, and, in one of those situations, may collaborate with the criminal. This happens, for example, with family disintegration.

19. *Resistant victim.* Does not accept aggression and thus reacts in defense of self or a third party, or also in fulfilling duty. Is always willing to fight against the aggressor.

20. *Victim of nature.* Is someone affected by a phenomenon of nature, such as an earthquake, flood or windstorm.

Henri Ellenberg (France, 1954)

1. *Criminal victim.* This person's conduct is directed both at the victim and the aggressor, as occurs with the drug dealer-addict.

2. *Latent victim or victim due to tendency.* Has a propensity, a special inclination of the personality towards being a victim.

Marvin Wolfgang (United States, 1956)

1. *Precipitating victims.* They provide, in some manner, support for the delinquent, precipitating the crime. Wolfgang researched cases of homicides in which there was provocation from the victims.

2. *Associated or collective victims.* They suffer as a group from the effects of criminal action. This would be the community who are victims of taxation and need derived from wrongful use of public moneys.

Willy Callewaert (France, 1959)

1. *Victim due to affective need.* This is a person of good faith, who becomes involved with the criminal. This victimization is typical with certain sexual partners who are led into crime.

2. *Victim due to one's own dishonesty.* Is gratified through conscious exposure to the effects of danger or damage from an assault by the author. Sometimes appears in fraud crimes.

Jean Pinatel (France, 1961)

1. *Determinant victim.* Due to personality disturbances, this person provokes disastrous consequences for him or herself, as has already been detected in investigations about ill-treatment or sexual abuses that led to parricide (murder of one's own father) or fratricide (murder of a sibling).

2. *Facilitating victim.* Arouses the author's appetite (*la victime eveille l'apetit*) by generating the occasion for the criminal act, as is evidenced in a crime of extortion or fraud. The crime of extortion, popularly known as *blackmail*, is characterized by the fact that the extortionist or black-mailer creates a situation of real constraint for the victim, such as demanding money in exchange for not divulging a compromising letter or photograph. In the practice of fraud, the delinquent plays on the victim's dishonest instinct of being attracted by profit or advantage, even if it exposes his or her dishonest attitude, as happens with the "Building Swindle," where apartments are sold several times and where the victim's bad faith in wanting to gain an advantage is evident, when she or he knows better than to be fooled by a proposed apartment price that is far lower than the market price.

3. *Socializable victim.* This is someone who is benefited by professional and scientific techniques in Pedagogy, Psychology and Psychiatry, which are directed towards finding mechanisms to allow the re-socialization and moral elevation of that victim in a social context.

Luiz Jimenez de Asua (Argentina, 1961)

1. *Indifferent or undefined victim.* The situation of quality of the person does not matter. He or she is chosen at random by the delinquent.
2. *Determined victim.* This person is chosen for a specific motive.
3. *Resistant victim.* Seeks to defend him or herself from the offender's action.
4. *Supporting victim.* In some way, he or she participates in practicing the crime, as in a duel and in assisted suicide.

Severin Versele (Belgium, 1962)

1. *Natural-born victim.* Constitutionally predestined to be a victim.
2. *Spontaneous victim.* In a given context exposes him or herself to victimization.
3. *Occasional victim.* Depending on the circumstance or conjecture, may become a victim.

Lola Aniyar de Castro (Venezuela, 1962)

1. *Singular or collective victim.* One or several persons.
2. *Victim of wrongdoing.* Suffers the action of a crime as defined by a law.
3. *Victim of oneself.* Self-victimizes.
4. *Victim due to tendency.* Reveals a personal inclination to be a victim.
5. *Repeat victim.* Suffers two or more victimizations.
6. *Habitual victim.* Permanently lives in a victimal situation.
7. *Professional victim.* Makes a living from being a victim.
8. *Culpose victim.* Imprudent, negligent or unskilled.
9. *Conscious victim.* Accepts undergoing a process of victimization, as a result of a situation in which he or she is fully conscious of the possibility of experiencing a victimal state. This would be the case of a mother throwing herself onto the road to avoid having her child hit by a car.
10. *Malicious victim.* Desires or expects to be a victim.

Torsten Sellin and Marvin Wolfgang (United States, 1964)

1. *Primary victim.* This is a certain person who suffers a particular or personalized victimization, as happens with malicious crimes against life.

2. *Secondary victim.* This is victimization of a specific group or part of the community, such as consumers.

3. *Tertiary victim.* Victimization directed against the whole community or population. This is a diffuse and generalized victim who appears in infractions involving the tax or financial order.

4. *Mutual victim.* This happens in cases where each participant may be victim and criminal, as occurs in scenes of homosexuality.

5. *Victim in a victimless crime.* The victim is a client of the author, and keeps silent because of that. Victimless crime is identified in cases of incest, drug addiction, abortion and usury.

Guglielmo Gulotta (Italy, 1971)

1. *False victim.* This is the *simulating victim,* in a situation in which an innocent person is accused, or an *imaginary victim,* who, in fact, suffers no damage or harm.

2. *Real victim.* This is the victim who will appear in one of the following hypotheses: accident, imprudence or voluntary provocation to crime.

Ezzat Fatah (Canada, 1971)

1. *Desirous or supplicant victim.* Desires or does anything to be victimized.

2. *Adhering victim.* Assumes the identification of empathy, friendship, understanding and esteem towards the aggressor's attitudes and behaviors. This is the *Stockholm Syndrome* phenomenon, which occurs, for example, with kidnap victims in captivity.

3. *Willing victim.* Even when not consenting, may in some way favor occurrence of the crime.

4. *Non-participating victim.* Repels the offender and the offense, in no way contributing to the origin of the offense.

5. *Latent of predisposed victim.* This person has a tendency or penchant for being a victim.

- *Biopsychological predisposition:* age, gender, physical state, alcoholism.
- *Social Predisposition:* profession, occupation, economic condition, social marginality.
- *Psychological Predisposition:* sexual deviancy, negligence, imprudence, character defect.

6. *Provoking victim.* Incites the criminal or sets the climate for the crime.

7. *Participating victim.* When the victim intervenes in the crime, adopting a passive attitude, facilitating action or aiding the author.

8. *False victim.* Victimizes him or herself or presents her or himself as victim of a crime, in which he or she had no involvement.

Vasile Stanciu (France, 1975)

1. *Victim from gestation or birth.* This person enters the world with an infirmity or traumatism suffered during the intrauterine life or during birth.

2. *Victim of the parents.* These are children in a victimal state of abuse.

3. *Victim of civilization.* This is someone who, in some manner suffers as a result of shock, mutations or transformations occurring, in a given period, in the characteristics of living in a certain Country or Society.

4. *Victim of the State.* When the State itself creates or furnishes situations for victims to arise.

5. *Victim of technological progress.* This is a person who, under some circumstance, suffers the effects of technological revolution, such as crimes practiced by means of information technology.

6. *Victim in a penal pairing.* This is victimization association with the understanding the aggressor reaches with the victim, but where each one has a distinct interest.

7. *Victim in a criminal pairing.* This is associated victimization, in which the aggressor's interests and those of the victim are homogenous in their form of expressing acquiescence to the crime.

The Penal Pairing may be converted into a Criminal Pairing, as in the cases of pimp and prostitute, incest, suicide pact.

Resulting from this association for victimization, there may be the appearance of a *Penal Third Party*, that is, the opportunist in the tragedy, who gains an advantage from the situation, sometimes even pretending to be a witness so as to harm of favor the delinquent or the victim.

Stephen Schafer (United States, 1977)

1. *Victim with no relation to the criminal.* This is the passive subject in the crime, because he or she has no link of commitment or connection with the delinquent.

2. *Provoking victim.* Always places him or herself into a state of imminent victimization.

3. *Biologically feeble victim.* This person has physical or mental problems.

4. *Socially feeble victim.* Is not well regarded in society.

5. *Self-victimizing victim.* Victim of him or herself.

6. *Political victim.* Suffers consequences because of his or her political ideas.

Hilda Marchiori (Mexico, 1980)

1. *Victim belonging to the family group.* This person suffers in some manner in the family environment.

2. *Victim known to the author.* The offender studies the person.

3. *Victim unknown to the author.* The offender acts on a given occasion, without worrying about the possibility of affecting an unknown person. This would apply to the victim of a stray bullet.

Elias Neuman (Argentina, 1984)

1. *Individual victim.* May be innocent, resistant, provoking, simulating or an accessory to the crime.

2. *Family victim.* A person who suffers in the family or domestic environment.

3. *Collective or community victim.* Group of persons jointly victimized by aggression or attempts in the community: rebellions, terrorism, genocide, drug traffic, illegal monopolies, frauds in urban planning, falsified medication or food, abuses by the government or economic power, fraudulent evasion of capital, censorship and abusive use of communications media.

4. *Victims of society or the social system.* Examples are: abandoned children, invalids, the sick, beggars, impoverished persons, the elderly, immigrants, ethnic and racial or religious minorities.

5. *Victims of the penal system.* An imprisoned person who begins to absorb the feeling of being a victim.

6. *Victim of an attack on territorial or institutional sovereignty.* Appears in situations such as invasion, nuclear barriers, forced extradition, embargoes and boycotts.

Jacques Verin (France, 1985)

1. *Individual victim.* A person individually considered the passive subject of a crime.

2. *Organizational victim.* Agencies, companies or institutions harmed by those seeking dishonest gain, illicit or undue advantage, such as occurs with the practice of "white-collar crime."

3. *Real victim.* The one on whom losses from the damage or offense fall.

4. *Apparent victim.* When the person affected passes on to a third party (apparent victim) the loss from the damage or the offense, exactly as happens with the consumer or client who pays for the products that are stolen from stores and supermarkets.

Ivan Jakovljevic (Yugoslavia, 1985)

1. *Victim of a crime typified in law.* This is the passive subject under Criminal Law.

2. *Accident victim.* Appears in traffic violations or work accidents.

3. *Victim of terrorism.* Coerced by terrorist action from a political movement or religious fanaticism.

4. *Victim of natural phenomena.* This happens in occurrences such as floods, drought, earthquakes and windstorms.

5. *Victim of armed conflict.* In situations of belligerency between peoples or communities.

Luis Rodriguez Manzanera (Mexico, 1988)

1. *Direct victim.* Victimization that affects a particular person.

2. *Indirect victim.* This is victimization by an oblique route, which affects a person who has a close relationship with the direct victim, as happens with rape and kidnapping, which affect the victim's family members.

3. *Known victim.* This is what becomes known to the population of to police and judicial authorities.

4. *Hidden victim.* This person remains anonymous, many times not even known to the criminal, as happens to victims of terrorist militias.

Edmundo Oliveira (Brazil, 1989)

1. *Programming victim.* When the victim sets up the arrangement that leads to a criminal action, assuming a clear role as actor, sometimes in an extraordinarily complex environment that sets in motion the crime that he or she has programmed, providing the means for involving a certain level of culpability, malicious or willful, for the person who is later accused as author of the crime.

Precipitating victim. When the victim joins or supports the action, contributing on some manner, with malice or guilt, to the action or omission of the offender in the process of executing or consummating the crime. As the French say *"la victime éveille l'apetit"* (the victim arouses the appetite), that is, becomes bait for the aggressor.

Forms of expressing the victim's *programming* or *precipitating,* according to the description of the typical conduct set in motion in a concrete case, are:

a. *Exclusively guilty victim.* This would be in a circumstance where the victim's conduct impedes the formation of a causal link that would justify an author's objective liability, with the resulting disappearance of the judicial reasons that could condemn the author under the limits of criminal justice, require him or her to make restitution under Civil Law, or impose any other sanction under some sort of administrative procedure.

b. *Concurrent victim.* This happens when there is intervention through the victim's conduct, which contributes towards subjective plurality characterized during execution of the infraction perpetrated by the author. This would be the case of concurrent liability in a banking establishment, which has the duty of indemnifying an account holder for pain and suffering because it made payment on a false or adulterated check.

c. *Reciprocally guilty victim..* He or she has a certain degree of liability because of a lack of caution and diligence in a given victimogenous situation. This would be the case with an account holder who facilitates, by omission, access to his or her checkbook that was used in falsification.

3. *Victim due to act of God.* This involves a person who suffers because of a phenomenon of nature or a calamity dictated by chance, when he or she is faced with a given fact that goes beyond the limits of human caution and the normal possibilities of prediction or predictability, which is the capacity or aptitude for foreseeing an occurrence. It is as if something walking down the street is struck by a lightning bolt, or, in another possibility, the disaster befalling a driver who becomes a victim when the seal connected to the steering wheel of the vehicle she or he is driving is broken. There is no crime to be punished, because there is no typical conduct due to malice or guilt.

4. *Victim of casus major.* In *casus major*, the person, without conditions for offering resistance, suffers from the effects resulting from pressure that is greater than the limits of his or her will and of behavior suggested by the moral sense. This would be the case of irresistible coercion that removes a person's psychic or physical freedom of exercising the will and free determination, such as in extreme situations in which he or she is seeking to guarantee survival, or in cases of clinical disturbances such as sleepwalking and hypnotically induced trance. There is no crime to be punished, because no typical conduct due to malice or guilt can be verified as being part of the act.

In conformity with what we have previously noted, in the approach to *victimal eventuality* as distinct from *victimal culpability*, *acts of God* and *casus major* require a supplementary explanation.

In penal dogmatics, the predominant thinking is in favor of the theory of objective imputation, in the sense that *acts of God* and *casus major* are factors that do not result in configuration of a criminal act, exactly because of the absence of malicious or culpable conduct. It is thus inferred that the interference of one of those factors (*act of God* or *casus major*) excludes culpability, related to the event, which was not motivated by the subject's intentions.

One must note, however, that *act of God* and *casus major* do not erase a possible characterization of the causal link, in the line that unfolds action going from human behavior to production of a result.

In relation to an *act of God,* on cannot deny, for example, this relation of causality, in the circumstance of a driver surprised by the rupture in brake pressure in his or her car brakes, leading to collision with a lamp post and the death of a pedestrian. In this case, a causal link is applicable, because had the driver not been driving the vehicle, the accident would not have occurred. What is excluded is recognition of human activity involving malice or guilt, considering that the behavior is atypical, and, since there is no infraction of conduct, obviously no value judgment will be issued on illicitness and culpability.

The same reasoning is juxtaposed in the use of *casus major*, as happened in the hinterland of the State of Bahia, when the head of a family, fleeing from drought, who after having given his children all of the water they had, overcome by thirst and without any other option, uncontrollably drank all of the cane rum in his canteen. Drunk, he lost control over his reflexes and, in a state of disorientation, wounded a friend with a knife. The relation of causality is relevant, since, had he not avidly consumed the alcoholic drink, he would certainly not have inflicted bodily harm on his traveling companion.

Gianluigi Ponti (Italy, 1990)

1. *Active victim*. Expresses a certain psychological attitude or mode of conduct that will influence the author's behavior. This is a person seeking stardom, and to make this dream a reality is willing to undergo inconveniences and dangerous adventures. This type of victim emerges, from time to time, in the world of the *top-models*.

2. *Passive victim* or *genuine victim*. This is a person in whom one does not see any objective or subjective manifestation for influencing or stimulating the origin or occurrence of the crime attributed to the author.

Chapter 11

Judicial Prosecution

Persecutio Criminis

Once a fact defined as a penal infraction has been committed, a situation of *jus puniendi* arises for the state, which is put into effect through a legal proceeding. Penal action serves exactly for deducing, in Court, the punitive intention of the State, so that the adequate penal sanction is applied, when *imputability* leads to *liability,* and that, for its part serves as a presupposition for gauging *culpability.*

A criminal suit brought by the Public Prosecution Service or by the offended party is known as the *persecutio criminis*, that is, mobilization for punishing the crime. Through this action there is an attempt to make the *jus puniendi* effective, in the sense of imposing upon the infractor the appropriate penal sanction as defined by law.

The Victim and the Penal Proceeding

The Argentinean professor Elias Neuman comments that, among the variables inherent to the behavior of a crime victim, the process of whether or not to bring charges against the delinquent is a noteworthy.[1] The victim always makes an assessment of the costs of this initiative to verify what it will represent in terms of real case, should he or she choose to go the court route. Alternative routes with lower losses, compared to the costs of formal justice, have contributed decisively towards the rate of evasion from the Court System (Neuman, 1994, p. 54).

In light of concrete facts that lead one to formulate a given hypothesis in which the victim precipitates or programs the coordinates of his and her own victimization, observation of facts leads to the conclusion that the victim, in some criminal occurrences, may not feel stimulated to seek formal levels of control (Police or Justice) due to the presence of factors that we will now enumerate.

- In the first place, the victim does not have a tranquil conscience (McDonald, 1976, p. 24), because he or she knows she or he is not totally innocent, with the degree of responsibility varying according to the scale of his or her concurrence with the crime;
- In the second place, the victim fears repercussions brought by press coverage, which might lead to people taking precautions against him or her, also considering that the Defense might drag her or his name through the mud;[2]
- In the third place, the victim knows that, in general, both the Police and the Courts are often slow and sometimes even ineffective in prosecuting and punishing the guilty (Castro, 1987, pp. 159-163).
- In the fourth place, the governments, with the exception of a few countries, have nothing or almost nothing to offer the victims in terms of assistance with their rights (Fragoso, 1977, pp. 19-20).
- In the fifth place, the victim has no expectations of receiving a fair value as indemnity for the damages caused (Bolle, 1989, pp. 53-55: Robert, 1990, pp. 90-93).

The motives that keep a victim from seeking protection and support from the Police, the Courts and Government social services[3] lead to the proliferation of victimacy zones, in which the high social level of the author of the infraction and the respect he or she enjoys in the community are utilized exactly to pressure victimization of persons from the lower social classes. In this manner, because of the strength of this power, the victim is lead to do or not do what he or she is ordered to due, either by coercion, or as a result of pseudo-tutelage or protection guaranteed by the delinquent. May of those victims frequently appear in wrongful actions linked, for example, to homosexuality, prostitution, drug use and gambling addiction.

Judith Becker wrote about this phenomenon, calling it the *dirty work syndrome*. Becker noted that "certain persons exhibit the credentials of morality due to the existence of a group of immoral people, who satisfy the moralists by doing what those persons like, but lack the courage to publicly exhibit."

Caught up in this scheme, the victim may be compelled into the role of "scapegoat." Thus, he or she becomes subject to the contingencies of a sort of *neutralization technique*, through which society excuses itself of the crime, blaming it on the depravity of the one who is the victim.[4] Criminal defense strategies are oriented towards exploiting those steroids, providing for the acquittal of quite a few defendants accused in criminal proceedings.

Notes

1. Elias Neuman remembers the victim's behavior that can contribute, cooperate or collaborate towards the outcome of the delinquent's attitude.

2. We may take as an example the client of a prostitute who always seeks her out privately, concerned with his reputation. If he should become the victim of robbery by the prostitute or her pimp, he will naturally not take his complaint to the police, because this would cause a scandal in his family environment and he does not want his social circle to know of his intimate involvement with a prostitute.

3. Jacques Verin, a French judge, published an interesting article praising government measures and activities of private associations for assisting victims in the United States, Germany, Poland, the United Kingdom and France (Verin, 1981, pp. 895-896).

4. *A Just World Theory,* written by Englishman Albert Lerner, is concerned with analyzing the data revealing the victim's responsibility (capacity for suffering censure) in acting as the personage who gives cause or provides decisive collaboration for the criminal event. The greater the judgment of reproof against the victim's behavior, the lesser should be the recognition of the delinquent's culpability (McDonald, 1976, p. 41

Chapter 12

The Victim in Brazilian Criminal Law

Generically, the focus on the victim in Brazilian criminal legislation employs normative prescriptions that focus on the quality or condition of someone who suffers or receives the consequences of an action or omission.

The Victim as Passive Subject

In terms of normative aspects, analysis of the victim, as a passive subject, encompasses the following hypothesis:

a. the limits of the relation between the author (active subject) and the victim (passive subject), considering the latter's qualities or personal conditions:
b. the nature of the interest or the asset legally protected by criminal law in relation to the victim;
c. the situation of the passive subject in regard to the subjective element of the crime, that is, of culpability;[1]
d. the performance of the passive subject in the process of the infraction, with his or her possible consent or concurrent guilt;
e. the role of the passive subject in relation to the conditions or circumstances of the crime, as happens with the causes for justifying the misdeed (legitimate defense, state of need, strict fulfillment of legal duty or regular exercise of law);

f. the passive subject in face of accessory elements or circumstances that influence the seriousness or mitigation of the crime's effects (increase of the sentence, reduction of the sentence or security measure);

g. the passive subject's conduct after the crime has occurred, regarding criminal proceedings, as in the cases of forgiveness, renunciation and retraction;

Various articles of the Penal Code contain references to the victim. We may observe, for example, the following provisions:

- art. 20, § 3—Error regarding the person;
- art. 25—Legitimate defense
- art. 45, § 1—Payment to the victim in cash;
- art. 59—Establishing the penalty;
- art. 61, II:

  c. aggravating circumstance due to the use of a recourse that makes defense by the offended party difficult of impossible;

  j. aggravating circumstance due to the agent taking advantage of a particular misfortune of the offended party;

- art. 65, III, c—extenuating circumstance due to violent emotion provoked by an unjust act of the victim;
- art. 105—Forgiveness by the offended party;
- art. 107:

  V—renunciation of the right to lodge a complaint;
  VII—marriage of the agent with the victim;

- art. 121, § 1—Malicious homicide shortly following unjust provocation by the victim;
- art. 121, § 2—Malicious homicide with a recourse that makes defense by the offended party difficult or impossible;
- art. 121, § 4—Malicious homicide with an increase in sentence, because the agent does not provide immediate help for the victim;
- art. 122—Inducement, instigation or aid in the suicide of someone;
- art. 129, § 4—Bodily harm with reduction of the sentence, due to unjust provocation by the victim;

- art. 140, § I—The Judge may forgo applying a penalty, if the offended party directly provoked the injury;
- art. 160—Direct extortion, abusing of someone's situation to give case for criminal proceedings against the victim;
- art. 220—Consensual abduction;
- art. 224—Statutory rape in sex crimes, when the victim is under 14 years of age, mentally alienated or deficient and also in the circumstance of the victim not being able to offer resistance;
- art. 227, § 1—Induce a victim older than 14 and younger than 18 to satisfy another person's lasciviousness.

Among the various normative dispositions of the Penal Code that make reference to the victim, the one that is of particular interest in the objective of our study is the one referring to **behavior of the victim**, this expression being contained in art. 59 of the Penal Code, which deals with establishing the sentence.

Art. 59. The judge, taking into account the agent's culpability, background, social conduct, personality, motives, the circumstances and consequences of the crime, as well as the victim's behavior, shall establish, as may be necessary, and sufficient for reproving and preventing crime:

I.   the applicable sentences among those that may apply;
II. the amount of the applicable sentence, within the limits provided for;
III. the initial regime for serving a sentence that denies freedom;
IV. substitution of a sentence that denies freedom for another type of sentence, if applicable.

The legislator explicitly included, among the judicial circumstances of art. 59 that influence calibration of the sentence, the behavior assumed by the victim.

It is the Exposition of Motives of the Penal Code (number 50), which devotes the greatest attention to the **delinquent-victim** duality when stating that "many times the victim's behavior is transformed into a criminogenous factor, because it constitutes provocation or stimulation towards criminal conduct."

We should also remember that the Special Section of the Penal Code provides some rules in which the victim's conduct acts as one of the causes implying penal effects. We may see, for example:

- art. 25—Exclusion of illicitness due to legitimate defense;
- art. 61, II, c, j—Circumstances aggravating the penalty;
- art. 65, III, c—Circumstance mitigating the penalty
- art. 121, § 1—Reduction of penalty due to justifiable homicide;
- art. 221—Reduction of the penalty in cases of kidnapping for the purpose of marriage;
- art. 224—Statutory rape in sex crimes, when the victim is under 14 years of age, mentally alienated or deficient and also in the circumstance of the victim not being able to offer resistance;
- art. 227, § 1—Increase of penalty for inducing a victim older than 14 and younger than 18 to satisfy another person's lasciviousness.

As Eduardo Mayr has emphasized (1990, p. 20), Brazilian criminal dogmatics has begun to show Judges that they must take into account the victim's gradation , from complete innocence to minimum, medium or maximum guilt.

Based on that scale of normative values, victimization must be assessed in consonance with the following groups:

a. innocent victimization;
b. conscious victimization;
c. unconscious victimization;
d. subconscious victimization.

Innocent Victimization

Innocent victimization appears in cases such as the death of the fetus in the crime of abortion.

Conscious Victimization

Conscious victimization is in regard to a clear notion of the manner of behavior in light of the act's illegal nature, because motivation for conduct operates in the field of memory perception. This would be the case with promotion of prostitution.

Unconscious Victimization

Unconscious victimization comes about with a conduct that possesses conflicts motivated by irrational forces that act outside of knowledge and memory. This is the case with sadomasochism, in which the person suffers aggression so as to have it culminate in sexual pleasure, without, nonetheless being conscious or realizing that the suffering, deep down, is the consequence of punishment of a guilt feeling, whose origin may have occurred in childhood.

Subconscious Victimization

Subconscious victimization is the case of a clouded mind, that is, a situation on the threshold between conscious and unconscious, which, due to an effort of memory, can lead the person to remember events occurring in moments of semiconsciousness. An example of this would be consumption of drugs, which puts the individual on the threshold of sleep and wakefulness.

In Brazilian Criminal Law the victim is never punished by the Criminal Judge; nonetheless, his or her behavior can influence in the gauging of the defendant's criminal liability and the appropriate sentencing. There has been a laudable evolution of Penal Science in absorbing the modern doctrines of Criminology and Victimology, which, since the end of World War II have been working to guarantee that Criminal Justice does not impose on the defendant the totality of consequences of a punishable fact, when the victim is also capable of contributing to characterization of the crime as a phenomenal reality.

It is interesting to note, opening up a parenthesis, that in Brazilian Law, indemnification for damages transcends Criminal Law, since the Criminal judge lacks powers to establish in the sentence any indemnification or reparation for the victim. It is Civil Law that receives suits for indemnification for physical, psychological or moral suffering that harms the victim. It would be desirable to establish indemnification for the victim, as reparation for damages, in the criminal sentence itself.

In the near future, with the advances of Victimology in the field of Law, art. 59 of the Penal Code will certainly speak of **behavior and**

diagnosis of the victim's personality, and not only in **behavior of the victim**.

It is more complete and secure to proceed with diagnosing a personality than to limit the image of behavior projected on the fact that is the object of the investigation. As we have demonstrated in the chapter on study of the personality, its components known as **temperament** and **character** are extremely important for gauging the victim's involvement in the criminal action, exactly because from the bases of these components, an imbalance in conduct may arise in any possible hypothesis of precipitation to crime, among the range of varieties of the victimological phenomenon.

Notes

1. There are three elements in the modern understanding of culpability; a) imputability, which makes it possible for the author to know that the fact practiced is contrary to duty; b) the psychological-normative element, which establishes the link between the conduct and the event, under the form of malice or guilt; c) requirement of adequate conduct regarding duty, which justifies later censure, because of violation of the law.

Conclusion

Here we conclude the critical examination of the highly relevant form-ulations resulting from significant advances in Victimology, espe-cially concerning technical and scientific investigations that involve the theme of **crime precipitated or programmed by the victim.**

It would be a great reward for this book to deserve consideration as a small starting point for studies that many offer greater creative capacity.

It is our hope that this work will strengthen the prestige of Criminal Law in the face of complexities involved in showing human beings that so much technological progress is worthless if we do not care for our-selves and do not aspire for holistic fulfillment of body and soul, so as to immerse ourselves in virtue and follow the optimal meaning of life.

At the very least, this book will provide a useful springboard for spirited debate among students, professionals, and members of the law enforcement, criminal justice and victim assistance communities.

Its most important use should be to sow seeds that help design and implement modern, harmonious policies for the treatment of delinquents and the control of crimes—policies that reflect increasingly enlightened attitudes and reactions.

Bibliography

ALEXANDER, F. *The Medical Value of Psychoanalysis,* New York, Norton, 1932.

ALIMENA, B. *I Limiti e Imodificatori Dell'Imputabilità,* Turim, EditoraFratelli Bocca, 1894.

ALLPORT, G. W. *Personalidade: Padrões e Desenvolvimento,* translated by Dante Moreira Leite, São Paulo, Ed. da Universidade de São Paulo, 1974.

ALTAVILLA, E. *O Delinqüente e a Lei Penal,* translated by Fernando de Miranda, Coimbra, Ed. Coimbra, 1964, vol. 2.

AMORIM, D. *Espiritismo e Criminologia,* Rio de Janeiro, EdiçõesCeld, 1993, vol. 2.

ANASTASI, A. *Tests Psicolócos,* Madri, Aguilar, 1980.

ANDRADE, M. C. *A Vítima e o Problema Criminal,* Coimbra, Ed. Coimbra, 1989.

ANDREAS, S. & ANDREAS, C. *A Essência de Mente,* São Paulo, Summus editorial, 1993.

ARNOUD, W. *Person, Charecter, Personlichkeit,* Müchen, Olzoy Verlay, 1975.

BARBE, E. *Curso de Filosofia,* Rio de Janeiro, Liv. Francisco Alves, 1915.

ABRIL, M. "L'Envers du Crime," *in Cahier du Centre International de Criminologie Comparée.* Montréal, Université de Montréal, 1984, pp.13-18.

BARKAN, S. E. *Criminology—A Sociological Understanding,* New Jersey, Prentice Hall, 1997.

BECKER, J. "Conventional Crime, Rationalization and Punish-ment," *in Sociological Work, Method and Substance,* Chicago, University of Chicago, 1970, p. 337.

BERARDINELLI, W. *Biotipologia: Constituição, Temperamento, Caráter,* Rio de Janeiro, Liv. Francisco Alves, 1936.

BETTIOL, G. *Direito Penal,* translated by Paulo José da Costa Júnior e Alberto silva Franco, São Paulo, Ed. Revista dos Tribunais, 1976, vol. 3.

BOLLE, P. H. "Le sort de la Victime des Actes de Violence Criminels en Droit Pénal Suisse," *in Criminologia y Derecho Penal al Servicio de la Persona,* San Sebastian, Universidad de San Sebastian, 1989, pp. 53-55.

CABANIS, P. *Du Rappot du Physique et du Moral de L' Homme,* Paris, Chevalier-Maresck, 1802.

CABRAL, A. & NICK E. *Dicionário Técnico de Psicologia,* São Paulo, Cultrix, 1974.

CALLEWAERT, W. "La Victimologie et L'Escroquerie," *in Revue de Droit Pénal et de Criminologie,* Paris, n° 2, 1959, pp. 613-615.

CANCIO MELIÁ, Manuel. *Conducta de la Victima e Imputación Objetiva en Derecho Penal.* Barcelona, Editorial Bosh, 1998.

CASANOVA, P. *Antropologia Jurídica,* Havana, Ed. Cultural, 1937.

CASTRO, L. A. *Criminologia de la Liberación,* Maracaibo, Universidad de Zulia, 1987.

———. *La Victimologia,* Maracaibo, Universidad del Zulia, 1969.

CLARKE, G. "A Lethal Delusion," *in Time, the Weekly Newsmagazine,* New York, 1980, n° 116, vol. 25, p. 21.

CODON, J. M. & SAIZ I. L. *Psiquiatria Jurídica Penal y Civil,* Burgos, Aldecor, 1968, vol. 1.

COLEMAN, J. C. *A Psicologia do Anormal e a Vida Contemporânea,* São Paulo, Pioneira, 1973.

CORNIL, P. "Contribuition de la Victimologie aux Sciences Criminologiques," *in Revuede Droit Pénal et de Criminologie,* Bruxelles, n° 2, 1959, pp. 589-601.

COSTA JUNIOR, P. J. *O Direito de Estar Só: Tutela Penal da Intimidade,* São Paulo, Ed. Revista dos Tribunais, 1970.

CUARON, A. Q. *Medicina Forense,* México, Editorial Porruá, 1980.

DAMPIER, W. C. *Histoire Général des Sciences,* Pais, Éditions Puf, 1957.

DASKALAKIS, E. *Réflexions sur la Responsabilité,* Paris, Éditions Puf, 1975.

DELGADO, Honório. *La Personalidad y Carater,* Barcelona, Editorial Científico Medina, 1966.

DENKERS, A. J. M. *Psychological Reactions of Victims of Crime: The Influence of Pre-Crime, Crime and Post-Crime Factors,* Amsterdam, Vrije Universiteit, 1966.

——. *La Personalidad y Carater,* Barcelona, Editorial Científico-Médica, 1996.

DEQUINCEY, T. *On Murder as one of the fine Arts,* London, *s.n., 1827.*

DETHLEFSEN, T. & DAHLKE, R. *A Doença como caminho,* translated by Zilda Hutchinson Schild, São Paulo, Ed. Pensamento, Cultrix, 1983.

DEWALD, Paulo. *Psicologia: Un enfoque Dinâmico,* Barcelona, Ediciones Toray, 1973.

DI TULLIO, B. *Pinrcípios da Criminologia Clinica y Psiquiatria Forense,* Madrid, Aguilar, 1963.

DIAMOND, S. *Personality and Temperament,* New York, Harper, 1957.

DIAS, J. F. *Direito Penal Português; as Consequências Jurídicas do Crime,* Lisboa, Acquitas, Ed. Notícias, 1993.

DIAS, J. F., ANDRADE, M. C. *Criminologia: o Homem Delinquente e a Sociedade Criminógena,* Coimbra, Ed. Coimbra, 1984.

DRAPKIN, I. "El Recluso Penal, Victima de la Sociedad Humana," *in Anuario de Derecho Penal y ciencias Penales,* Madrid, Edición de la Universidad, 1977, pp. 345-350.

EYSENCK, H. *Crime and Personality,* Columbia, Foreword, 1978.

FATTAH, Ezzat. "Victims Rights: Past, Present and Future. A global View," *in Oeuvre de Justice et Victimes,* vol. 1, Paris, l'Harmattan Sciences Criminelles, 2001, pp. 63-81.

FERRI, E. *Archivio di Psichiatria,* Turim, Editore Bocca, 1880, vol. 1.

——. *Sociologia Criminale,* Turim, Ed. Utet, 1929, vol. 1.

FORTES, H. & PACHECO, G. *Dicionário Médico,* Rio de Janeiro, F. Melo Editor, 1968.

FRAILE, G. *Historia de la Filosofia en Grécia y Roma,* Madrid, Biblioteca de Autores Cristianos, 1971.

FRAGOSO, H. *Direito Penal e Direitos Humanos,* Rio de Janeiro, Ed. Forense, 1977.

FRANÇA, L. *Noções de História da Filosofia,* São Paulo, Companhia Editora Nacional, 1943.

FREEDMAN, A.; KAPLAN, H.; SADOCK, B. *Compêndio de Psiquiatria,* translated by Jorge Freixas e Antônia Grimalt, Barcelona, Salvat, 1975.

FREUD, S. *La TécnicaPscoanalítica,* Madrid, Biblioteca Nueva, 1968, vol. 3

———. *El Yo e el Ello,* Madrid, Biblioteca Nueva, 1968, vol. 2.

FROASALI, R. A. "Il Delinquente der Tendenza nel Diritto Positivo," *in Studi in Memoria di Arturo Rocco,* Milão, 1952, vol. 1, p. 450.

GARRAUD, R. *Traité de Droit Pénal Français,* Paris, L. Larouse, 1935, t. 6.

GAROFALO, R. *Criminologia,* translated by Julio de Mattos, Lisboa, Liv. Clássica Editora, 1916.

GEIS, G. *Victimization Patterns in White Collar Crime. Victimology,* London, University Edition, 1961.

GEIWITZ, J. P. *Teoria não Freudiana da Personalidade,* São Paulo, Pedagógica e Universitária, 1973.

GEMELLI, A. *La Personalità del Delinquente;* Milano, Dott A. Giuffrè Editore, 1948.

———. *La Personalità del Delinquente; Nei Suoi Fondamenti Biologici e Psicologici, 2ª ed. ,* Milão, Dott. A. Giuffrè Editore, 1948.

GOFFMAN, E. *Stigma Notes on the Management of Spoiled Identity,* Penguin, Belmont, 1976.

GONZAGA, J. B. *O Direito Penal Indígena à Época do Descobrimento do Brasil,* São Paulo, Max Linonad Editor, 1972.

GÖPPINGER, H. *Criminologia,* translated by Maria Luiza Schuwarch e Ignácio Luzarraga Castro, Madrid, Instituto Editorial Reus, 1975.

GOULDNER, A. *La Crisis de la Sociologia Occidental,* Buenos Aires, Paidos, 1973.

HENTING, H. *The Criminal and his Victim,* Yale, University Press, 1948.

———. *Estudios de Pscologia Criminal,* Madrid, Espasa Calpe, 1962.

HINDELANG, H., GOTTREDSON. M. & GAROFALO, J. *Victims of Personal Crime: an Empirical Foundation for a Theory of Personal Victimization,* Cambridge, Edition Ballinger, 1978.

HORÁCIO, Q. *Ouevres Complètes,* Paris, Garnier, 1950, vol. 2.

INGENIEIROS, J. *Princípios de Pscologia,* Boenos Aires, Rosso y Cia., 1919.

JANET, P. *Traité de Phisolophie,* Paris, Delagrave, 1944.

JIMENEZ DE ASÚA, L. "La Llamada Victimologia," *in Estudios de Derecho Penal y Criminologia"* Buenos Aires, 1961, vol. I, pp. 19-31.

KAHN, F. *O Corpo Humano,* São Paulo, Civilização Brasileira, 1943, vol. 2.

KENPIS, T. *Imitação de Cristo,* Rio de Janeiro, Agir, 1970.

KOFFKA, K. *Principles of Gestalt Psychology.* New York, Harcourt, 1933.

LAHR, C. *Cours de Philosophie,* Paris, Gabrielle Bouchesne, 1926, vol. 1.

LANGELÜDDEKE, A. *Psiquiaytria Forense,* translated by Luis Beneytez Merino, Madrid, Editorial Espasa, Calpé, 1972.

LINS E SILVA, C. *A Defesa Tem Palavra,* Rio de Janeiro, Aide, 1984.

LOMBROSO, C. *L'Uomo Delinquente,* Torino, Fratelli Bocca, 1876.

LOPEZ, G. *Victimologie,* Paris, Edition Dalloz, 1977.

POPEZ, G. & BORNSTEIN, S. *Victimologie Clinique,* Paris, Édition Maloine, 1995.

LOPEZ-REY. A. *Criminologia,* Madri, Aguilar, 1978, vol. 2.

LUKESCH, A. *Mito e Vida dos Índios Kaiapó,* São Paulo, Ed. da Universidedade de São Paulo., 1976.

LUNDIN, R. W. *Personalidade,* São Paulo, Pedagógica e Universitária, 1977.

MANVELL, R. ; PRAENKEL, H. *Le Crime Absolu,* Paris, Stock, 1968.

MANZANERA, L. R. *Victimologia,* México, Editorial Porruá, 1988.

MANZINI, V. *Tratatto di Diritto Penale Italiano, Turim, Unione Tipografico Editrice Torinese, 1959, vol. 3.*

MAZON, S. F. *História da Ciência,* translated by José Vellinhho de Lacerda, Porto Alegre, Ed. Globo, 1957.

MAURACH, R. *Tratado de Derecho Penal,* translated by Córdoba Roda, Barcelona, Ariel, 1962, vol. 2.

MAYR, E. "Atualidade Vitimológica," *in Vitimologia em Debate,* Rio de Janeiro, Ed. Forense, 1990.

McDONALD, W. *Criminal Justice and the Victim,* London, University Edition, 1976, vol. 6.

MENACHEN, A. *Victim Precipitated Forcible Rape,* Chicago, University of Chicago, 1967.

MENDELSOHN. B. "Victimologia y las Tendencias de la Sociedad Contemporanea," *in Ilanud al Dia,* San José, 1981, n° 10, pp. 59-60.

MENDOZA, J. R. "Los Aspectos de la Prevención em los Delitos Culposos de Automobilismo em Relación com la Victima del Accidente," *in Revistade Defesa Social Nueva,* Caracas, 1953, n° 1, p. 43.

MIDDENDORF, W. "The Offender—Victim Relationship as far as Traffic Offenses are Concerned." *In Symposium on Victimology,* Jerusalém, University Edition, 1973, pp. 119-123.

MONTERO, Andrés. "Shaping the Etiology of the Stockholm Syndrome: Hypothesis of the Induced Mental Model," *in Iber Pscologia,* Valencia, 1999, vol. 5, n° 1, pp. 4-5.

MORA, J. F. *Diccionário de Filosofia,* México, Atlante, 1941.

MUNN, N. *Psychology: The Fundamentals of Human Adjustment,* Boston, Riverside Press Cambridge, 1951.

NEUMAN, E. *Victimologia, El Rol de la Victima em los Delitos Convencionales,* Buenos Aires, Edición de la Universidad, 1994.

NUVOLONE, P. "La Victime dans la Genèse du Crime," *in Études Internacionales de Psycologie Sociologie Criminele,* Paris, n°s 26-28, 1975, p. 50.

OLIVEIRA, E. *O Crime Precipitado pela Vítima,* Belém, Cejup, 1988.

———. *Comentários ao Código Penal,* Rio de Janeiro, Ed. Forense, 2005.

PALMIERI, V. M. *Medicina Forense,* Nápoles, Morano, 1964, vol. 2

PEASE, Ken. "Repeat Victimisation: Taking Stock," *in Crime Prevention,* London, Home Office, 1998, pp. 90-92.

PEASE, Ken e FARREL, Grahan, "Once Bitten, Twice Bitten: Repeat Victimisation and its Implications for Crime Prevention," *in Crime Prevention.* London, 1993, Home Office, 1993, p. 46.

PIEDADE JÚNIOR, H. *Vitimologia: Evolução no Tempo e no Espaço,* Rio de Janeiro, F. Bastos, 1993.

PINATEL, J. "Les Aspects Interpersonnels de la Conduit Criminelle," *in Revue de Science Criminelle et de Droit Pénal Comparé,* Paris, n° 2, 1961, pp. 342-344.

POKORNY, A. *A Comparison of Homicides in Two Cities,* Houston, University of Houston, 1965.

QUINNEY, R. *Who is the Victim?,* New York, University of New York, 1972.

RELAZIONE MINISTERIAL AL PROGETTO DEFINITIVO DEL CODICE PENALE. Roma, Tipografia Ufficiale, 1929.

REVISTA ISTO É. São Paulo, n° 1666, 2001.

RINPOCHE, S. *O Livro Tibetano do Viver e do Morrer,* translated by Luiz Carlos Lisboa, São Paulo, Ed. Talento, 1999.

ROBBINS, A. *Poder sem Limites,* Translated by Muriel Alves Brazil, São Paulo, Ed. Best Seller, 1987.

ROBERT, P. "Connaitre la Demarche Sociale un Préalable a Toute Politique em Faveur des Victimes," *in L'Indenisation des Victimes de la Violence*, Paris, Ministèrs de la Justice, 1990, pp. 90-93.

SAMPSON, Alice & PHILLIPS, Coretta. "Multiple Victimization: Radical Attacks on an East London Estate," *in Crime Prevention*, London, Home Office, 1992, pp. 36.

SCHIFFERES, J. *Enciclopédia Médica*, Rio de Janeiro, Record, 1964.

SCHNEIDER, H. J. *Kriminologie*, Berlin, Walter de Gruyter & CO., 1987.

————. "The Position of the Victim in Criminal Law and Procedure," *in Victimology*, Zagrelo, Separovic Editor, 1988.

SCHNEIDER, K. *Ligações de Psiquiatria para Médicos*, translated by Fernando Ferreira, São Paulo, Ed. Liv. Acadêmica Saraiva, 1936.

————. *Psicopatologia Clínica*, translated by Emanuel Carneiro Leão, São Paulo, Ed. Mestre Jou, 1976.

SEELING, E. *Traité de Criminologie*, Paris, Édition Puf, 1956.

SHAPIRO, S. *A Background paper on White Collar Crime*, Yale, University of Yale, 1976.

SIGHELE, S. *La Coppia Criminale*, Torino, Frateli Bocca, 1982.

SILVERMAN, R. "Victim Typologies," in *Victimology*, Lexington, Lexington Books, 1975.

SKINNER, B. F. *The Behavior of Organisms*, New York, University Press, 1938.

SOLJENITZYN, A. *Arquipélago Gulag*, translated by Francisco Ferreira, Márcia Ilisto & José Seabra, São Paulo, Círculo do Livro, 1973.

STANCIU, V. V. *Les Droits de la Victime*, Paris, Édition Puf, 1985.

STRENTZ, T. *The Stockholm Syndrome:* Law Enforcement Policy and Hostage Behavior. In Ochberg, F.M. and Soskis, P.A., eds. *Victims of Terror*, Boulder, Colorado, Westview Press, 1982.

SUTHERLAND, E. *The Professional Thief*, Chicago, University of Chicago, 1937.

————. *White Collar Crime* , New York, University of New York, 1961.

SYKES, G. M. *El Crimen y la Sociedad*, translated by Elizabeth Gelin, Buenos Aires, Paidos, 1961.

SYMONDS, Martin. *The Second Injury: Evaluation and Change*, New York, Criminal Justice Press, 1980.

TABONE, M. *A Psicologia Transpessoal*, São Paulo, Ed. Cultrix, 1993.

TARDE, G. A. *A Filosofia Penal*, Paris, Édition Puf, 1980.

TELLES JUNIOR, G. *O Direito Quântico,* São Paulo, Max Limonad, 1974.

VAN DIJK, J. J. M. *Attitudes of Victims and Repeat Victims Toward the Police: Results of the International Crime Survey,* New York, Criminal Justice Press, 2001.

————. *Criminal Victimization and Victim Empowerment in an International Perspective,* New York, Criminal Justice Press, 2001.

VARGAS, H. S. *Periculosidade Vitimal,* Londrina, Edição Universitária, 1989.

VERIN, J. "Uni Politique Criminelle Fondée sur la Victimologie et sur l'Intérêt des Victimes," *in Revue de Sicience Criminelle et de Droit Pénal Comparé,* Paris, 1981, n° 4, pp. 895-896.

VERNET, R. *Chromosomes et Criminalité,* Paris, Edition Études, 1968.

VERSELE, S. C. *Appunti di Diritto e di Criminologia com Riguardo alle Victime dei Delitti en la Scuola Positiva,* Milano, Giuffrè, 1962, n° 4, pp. 593-604.

WEMMERS, Jo-Anne. *Introduction à la Victimologie,* Montrèal, 2003.

WINER, Jonathan M. *Globalization, Terrorist Finance and Global Conflict, in Financing Terrorism,* London, Kluwer Academic Publishers, 2002, pp. 23-26.

WOLFGANG, M. "Victim Precipitated Criminal Homicide," *in Journal of Criminal Law, Criminology and Police,* New York, 1957, vol. 48, pp. 9-11.

————. *Victim Precipitated Criminal Homicide,* Philadelphia, University of Philadelphia, 1957.

WUNDT, W. *Psicologia Fisiológica,* Barcelona, Salvat, 1952.

ZOHAR, D. *O ser Quântico,* translated by Maria Antonia Van Acker, São Paulo, Ed. Best Seller, 1990.

Index

About the Author

Edmundo Oliveira is Professor of Criminal Law and Criminology at the University of Amazonia, Brazil.

He received his Ph.D. from the Federal University of Rio de Janeiro, Brazil. He also obtained the Post-Doctoral Degree Studies at the University of Paris, France, and realized important scientific research about alternatives to prison at University of Miami School of Law.

In the international arena, Professor Oliveira has been developing technical juridical-scientific activities and has provided expert services related to the following prestigious institutions:

Chairman of the National Council of Criminal Politics and Penitentiary of Brazil, 1991-1995;

Full Member of the Superior College of the Highest Chamber of Latin American Jurists, Argentina, since 2004;

Member of the International Penal and Penitentiary Foundation, created by the General Assembly of the United Nations, Switzerland, since 1997;

Member of the Board of Directors and Vice-President for Latin America of the International Society of Criminology, Counselor body of the United Nations and European Council, France, since 1990;

Scientific Consultant for the European Institute of the United Nations for Crime Prevention and Control, Finland, since 2005;

Advisor to the Committee for the Organized Crime Observatory, Switzerland, since 2004;

Member of the American Society of Criminology, United States, since 2007;

Coordinator of the International Department of the US-PIT Law Enforcement Training at Orlando, Florida, United States, since 2005.

Author of several books and articles in the field of Criminal Science, he has received many foreign awards and has been invited to lecture and speak at various Universities on every continent.

In the etymological essence of the word, Professor Oliveira is a complete *jurist*, considering that the real jurist is one who offers an original contribution to the science of law.